The
Great Sicilian
Cat Rescue

D0278009

The Great Sicilian Cat Rescue

ONE ENGLISHWOMAN'S MISSION TO SAVE AN ISLAND'S CATS

JENNIFER PULLING

JOHN BLAKE

Published by John Blake Publishing Ltd,
3 Bramber Court, 2 Bramber Road,
London W14 9PB, England

www.johnblakebooks.com

www.facebook.com/johnblakebooks
twitter.com/jblakebooks

This edition published in 2015

ISBN: 978 1 78418 378 3

All rights reserved. No part of this publication may be reproduced, stored in a
retrieval system, or transmitted in any form or by any means, without the prior
permission in writing of the publisher, nor be otherwise circulated in any form
of binding or cover other than that in which it is published and without a similar
condition including this condition being imposed on the subsequent purchaser.

British Library Cataloguing-in-Publication Data:

A catalogue record for this book is available from the British Library.

Design by www.envydesign.co.uk

Printed in Great Britain by CPI Group (UK) Ltd

3 5 7 9 10 8 6 4

© Text copyright Jennifer Pulling 2015

The right of Jennifer Pulling to be identified as the author of this
work has been asserted by her in accordance with the
Copyright, Designs and Patents Act 1988.

Papers used by John Blake Publishing are natural, recyclable products made from
wood grown in sustainable forests. The manufacturing processes conform to the
environmental regulations of the country of origin.

Every attempt has been made to contact the relevant copyright-holders,
but some were unobtainable. We would be grateful if the
appropriate people could contact us.

To my father, George, who taught me cats
were created to be cherished.

Contents

Prologue

I am standing in a Sicilian bus park, waiting for a man I have never met before. We are to drive along narrow twisting roads to a small town in the mountains in search of a badly injured cat. It is a balmy evening in June 2002, the air laden with the sensuous fragrance of jasmine, which steals into my mind and conjures up images of my past in this little town of Taormina. A shawl of magenta bougainvillea is slung over the wall to my left, while swallows dart through the dusky sky.

There is a voluptuousness of the senses about Sicily; you forget you are no more than a twenty-minute ferry ride from the toe of Italy. Perhaps its history of invaders – Arab, Norman and Phoenician to name but a few, each leaving their stamp on the landscape – gives this island its sense of otherness.

From the *trattoria* a few yards down the road come the tantalising scents of garlicky tomato and basil. I imagine the tables packed with holidaymakers enjoying their meal. Drunk on sunshine, a day spent basking like lizards on the beach at Isola Bella or Mazzaro, they throw off their northern reticence, speak in loud voices, call for another carafe of the local wine. Gales of laughter, they haven't a care in the world. How my stomach growls! I would love to be among them, forking up chunks of aubergine, savouring the rich sauce of *Pasta alla Norma* with its sprinkling of smoked ricotta. Or maybe I would choose *Pasta con le Sarde*, the dish that derives from Arabic cuisine, with its combination of sultanas, pine nuts and saffron. Yet the ingredients themselves have been native to Sicily since the time when the Greeks first landed on Naxos beach and settled there. Wild fennel comes into it and anchovy fillets, as well as the ubiquitous sardines.

Buses roar in and out of this park while I wait, musing on food. The airport coach disgorges new arrivals; a young woman with red hair tears herself from the arms of a young man and boards, waving desperately as the vehicle bears her away. It reminds me that my stay in Taormina, unlike those other times, is limited.

I ask myself: What am I doing here, bound on this mission with only a faint hope of finding the poor creature? Who knows, by now it may have run off to hide and die. Why can't I simply enjoy this beautiful evening? But that is my nature: always divided by a sense of duty and a rage to live. I am poised between staying and going. If this man doesn't arrive soon…

A car swings into the bus park; the man at the wheel calls out my name. It is Giulio.

x

ONE

A Cat
Called Lizzie

What I didn't know at that time was where this rescue of a small cat, white with smudges of black, would lead me. Perhaps it was just as well for I was about to embark on a journey that has already stretched over twelve years with no end in sight. It has been one of hard work and many obstacles but also success, and on the way I have changed from that person with her overly romantic view of Sicily. She, that other Jenny, with her very different vision of this island, now seems remote. My eyes have been opened to another, shadowy side of the place I believed I knew so well.

That morning, as we sat with our coffee, my friend and travelling companion Andrew and I, gazing down from the apartment's picture window onto Isola Bella, I could never have imagined how the day would turn out. From our eyrie, 250 metres above the coast, people looked like ants crawling over the isthmus, a narrow path of sand connecting the rocky island to the mainland, constantly shaped and reshaped by currents and tides. Taormina is perched on the side of the rocky Monte Tauro and so we had a wonderful view of the bay nestled between two high cliffs. The northern one, Capo Sant'Andrea, with its famed Blue Grotto, shelters the bay from northeast and east winds; the southern one, Capo Taormina, screens west winds. The jewel they encircle is a painter's paradise of ever-changing light. This morning it was magnificent, with the sun spread like molten silver over the sea so that one side of the island was in deep shadow, the other luminous.

Yesterday evening, as we made the steep walk back, pausing every now and again to regain our breath before we took another flight of steps, the light was limpid, pearl grey and pink; you could see quite clearly the outline of Calabria, the lights twinkling at the ferry port of San Giovanni. The island seemed afloat in translucent mist while a strange-looking sun hovered and then set, and the sea towards Messina had a glassy surface.

I revelled in the thought that this view would be mine for six weeks. If I had had any misgivings about my prolonged stay in Taormina, they vanished the first time I stepped into this apartment. It was gorgeous: its great bed dressed with flowery coverlets and cushions, the bathroom stacked with fluffy towels, and there was plenty of hot water. The kitchen was efficiently equipped with microwave, cooker, refrigerator and a cupboard full of every possible cleaning material I might need. My German landlady, Elke, had thought of everything. But the most delightful thing was this huge, wonderful window giving onto Isola Bella.

I could have sat there all day, reading or writing, sometimes raising my head to see the way the water crept across the peninsula. I would watch time pass from morning when the sun rises scarlet over the little island to night and the moon silvering the sea, where one or two fishing boats might be seen.

Andrew interrupted my thoughts. 'What shall we do today?'

I considered. It was a long time since I'd sat in the Bar Turrisi and sipped a glass of *Vino di Mandorla*, beginning with the first sweetness but developing into the bitter and characteristic taste of almond.

'I know, let's take the bus up to Castelmola,' I suggested. 'You've never seen it, have you? And there's a very odd place I want to show you.'

I have said that the views from Taormina are beautiful, but those from Castelmola, a natural balcony above it, are even more spectacular. You gaze down over the hills and valleys, traced with snaking pathways, and the faint tinkle of goats' bells floats through the still air. On a clear day you can see not only Etna but as far as Syracuse and Augusta along the Ionian coast, even the coastline of mainland Calabria.

The town is a place of lava stone-paved piazzas, a maze of small winding streets, where often there seems no sign of life apart from the cats scurrying away at your approach. You'll maybe catch a whiff of lunch being prepared, frying fish perhaps, and always the scents of basil and garlic. Along the main street, Via de Gasperi, there remains the sense of stepping back in time; there are no cars in central Castelmola. Here you can buy lace and embroideries made by the local women, who sit outside their shops and call out to friends as they pass. Then there are the armoured and glaring marionettes for sale, the *pupi* belonging to an oral tradition handed down from father to son. I once went to a puppet theatre in Catania. The performance was all clashing swords and declamations. My companion told me that the theme was based on a Frankish romantic poem, the 'Song of Roland' perhaps or 'Orlando Furioso', but I have to admit I didn't understand a word of it.

We had arrived in Piazza San Antonio where, years ago, I sat in the Bar Giorgio on a chilly winter's day, feeling I had somehow strayed into an alpine village. I almost expected to hear yodelling. About me there was a murmur of voices, the Sicilian dialect, which I never succeeded in mastering, except for the odd few words and phrases. '*Muh*' is one of them, that ever-present expression accompanied by a shrug of the shoulders, which can mean so many things: 'I don't know', 'What can one do?', even 'I'm not telling you anything'. Then there is *pazienza*, which sums up the resignation to fate of these islanders, whether the passing of a husband or the dreaded hot and humid wind that blows in from the Sahara, the Sirocco.

There seemed to be no other foreign visitors at that time of year and Castelmola was almost deserted; only about a thousand people live there permanently. My table was an oasis amid all that impassioned conversation where, as always, I was busily writing.

But today the goal was Bar Turrisi. I wanted to surprise Andrew with its bizarre collection. Phallus images of every size, shape and colour crowd the place – on counter tops, carved into stair railings and chairs, hung on the walls and drawn on the menu. Visit the bathroom and you will find yourself washing your hands under a tap shaped like a male

4

member. The obvious symbol is fertility and the bar owner's boast of procreating three sons in five years lays claim to that.

The sun burned in the vivid blue sky, reflected off the paving, and I could think of nothing I should like more than to sit in the dim, cool depths of Bar Turrisi with a glass of that ice-cold wine.

But Andrew hesitated. 'Later,' he said.

And he was off, darting down some steps that led to a lower level, while I in my heeled sandals followed more cautiously, through the narrow, uneven streets of this labyrinthine village. Here, one street looks very much like another, the front doors of the houses giving directly onto them, and we seemed to be going round in a circle. I paused to admire a window box stuffed with gaudy geraniums and lost sight of Andrew. When I did catch up, I found he had halted and was staring in silence.

'What? What is it?'

And then I saw. Lying on the ground was a small black and white cat with a ghastly wound – a back leg so shattered we could see the bone protruding through its skin. We couldn't understand why the fur surrounding the wound was stained with what looked like a pink dye. She did not move, in the way of cats enduring without a sound what must have been considerable pain.

'We've got to do something,' I said.

I glanced upward. At that moment a group of local people passed along the street above us, speaking in loud voices.

They halted and peered down. 'Poor creature,' I heard one of them say but then they moved on.

'What can you do?' asked Andrew.

'Something,' I replied firmly. 'We can't just leave her like this.'

I went up the steps again and scanned the road for any sign of a human being. It was now deserted. Then as I turned into another small street I saw a young man in the forecourt of a house, working on his motorbike. I hurried across.

'Can you help? I need to find a vet, there is a badly injured cat over there.'

He was a big, beefy young man, wearing a black leather jacket. I expected him to laugh or just turn away, but he listened to me.

'I know a vet,' he said. 'But he isn't from here. If you like, we can call him on my phone.'

That was the moment I first spoke to Giulio. No, he couldn't come at the moment – he was working with farm animals in the centre of Sicily but he would be in the vicinity later on. If I liked, we could return to Castelmola around eight, that night, and see what he could do.

I went back to tell Andrew. The cat in the fastidious way of felines had been trying to clean herself. I wondered again about the pink dye staining her fur. There was no question now of going to Turrisi to enjoy that almond wine. We hung around, eyeing the wretched creature, feeling helpless. Time passed.

Andrew glanced at his watch. 'The bus is due in ten minutes,' he said, 'we'd better get going.'

By now I was crying.

'I'm not leaving her,' I told him.

'If we don't catch this one, it will have to be the next because it's the last and there's no other way of getting back to Taormina. What can you do until the vet can come?'

He was right, of course. With one last look at the poor creature, I tore myself away and we hurried through the streets to the bus stop. The sunlit, carefree sense of Castelmola seemed replaced by gloom: it had become a hostile place where people could leave a small cat to suffer.

Back at the apartment, we sat at the window with a glass of wine, waiting for the time to pass until I could go back to the bus park, where Giulio had arranged to meet me.

If he thought I was a mad Englishwoman, he made no comment; perhaps in this tourist town he was used to it. He had come prepared with a torch, thick gauntlets and a humane cat trap. We took the winding road again, back to Castelmola.

Night falls suddenly in Sicily. Pools of light lay over the streets from the cafes and restaurants where people laughed and talked, darting a curious glance at the man and woman hurrying past, carrying a trap and a torch. I felt disorientated as we prowled the little streets, trying to find the one where I'd last seen her. Was it these steps or those? It was hard to tell in the gloom. Beginning to lose hope, I was afraid that Giulio would grow impatient and suggest we abandon our search but he seemed to be equally determined to find her.

At last he snapped off his torch. 'She is probably hiding,' he said. 'Let's go to that restaurant and ask for some food to put in the trap.'

'*Muh!*' said the proprietor but nevertheless he handed over a small tin of meat. We set it in the trap and moved away to hide round a corner, to watch and wait. It must have been almost half an hour later when we heard the release of the trap door. We rushed over and there was a small black and white cat, scrabbling at the wire bars, frantic to escape. Then we drove down to Giulio's surgery in Giardini.

Giardini… the name has such resonance for me. It was here

7

at the station that I arrived for the first time in Sicily, thirty years ago. Candelabra hang from its marvellous booking-hall ceiling, an exquisite piece of art deco.

Cunningly disguised as Bagheria on the western side of Sicily, the station featured in the film *Godfather III*. Here, Michael Corleone awaited his wife and children, who were visiting for his son Anthony's debut in *Cavalleria Rusticana*.

Giardini station is the gateway to the north; from here you can travel directly to Milan or Venice, but when I arrived it was from Rome. When I step inside, I see again the young girl climbing down from the train with her suitcase, bemused after so many hours' travel, who finds the station cafe and drinks her first cup of Sicilian coffee with the scent of harsh cigarette smoke in her nostrils.

Tonight, however, we stood in Giulio's surgery under the brilliant neon light while the cat, released from the trap, flew demented round the room, even up the walls, searching for escape.

Giulio burst out laughing and I joined in. 'What are we doing?' he asked.

Somehow he managed to grab hold of the cat and give her a sedative, then I went to sit in the little waiting room while he set and plastered the break. I stared at the clock on the wall: it was eight hours since we had taken that fateful turning in Castelmola. *Why hadn't we stuck to my plan?* I asked myself. We might be standing in Taormina's Piazza IX Aprile by now, gazing over to the red glow of Etna, that moody volcano, as every Sicilian feels drawn to do, at least once a day. But I knew my answer: it seemed fate had taken us down that narrow street perhaps hours after a vehicle had struck the little cat. Had it been anyone else I doubt they would have bothered, if the attitude of those passing Sicilians was anything to go by. But I had made up my mind: whatever it cost, I was prepared to do all I could to restore her.

'What was that pink stuff?' I asked Giulio when he finally emerged, carrying the cat now safely secured in a basket.

'Bleach,' he replied. 'Some mistaken idiot thinking it would disinfect the wound.'

'They don't seem to understand anything about animals here,' I observed.

Giulio gave the '*muh*' shrug.

The question was: what now? The cat couldn't stay here, that was obvious, so where? Scarcely thinking what I was saying, I told Giulio I would nurse her in the apartment.

He gave me a wry smile. 'For at least two weeks! Are you sure?'

I sighed. 'What else can I do?'

It was almost midnight when we arrived back at the apartment and I rang the outside doorbell. Andrew came hurrying down the steps.

'What's going on?' he asked.

Giulio shook my hand. 'I must go, but I'll call by in a few days' time to see how she is getting on,' he told me before disappearing down the little street.

'I'm going to call her Lizzie,' I said, as Andrew carried the cat basket up to the apartment door. 'Because she is my queen of Castelmola.'

'You're mad,' he told me.

TWO

A Romantic's View of Italy

I can see clearly where my love affair with Sicily began: I spent my teenage years reading about life while my peers were out experiencing it. Illness constrained me to live vicariously through the novels of E.M. Forster, Henry James, Flaubert and Tolstoy.

There was Daisy Miller who flirts with the unsuitable moustachioed Italian and, defying the warnings of her sensible relatives, succumbs to malaria after staying up all night with him in the Forum. Then there was Emma Bovary and Anna Karenina. The lesson I learned from these stories was that, even if experience proved fatal in one sense or another, it must be submitted to.

I wrote – and published – women's magazine short stories. In all of them providence stepped in, disappointments were overcome and a solution offered, though often that solution was to move on after a transient love affair. All this was hardly the best preparation for success in the eyes of the world but such tales of women who defied common sense and pursued their lust for life persuaded me it was necessary to sacrifice all for romance. Worse, I also believed there was some destiny or fate that would take over and guide me; I just had to get myself out there and see what happened.

At twenty-two, I was completely recovered and ready to dive in, in short, to live! But where? And how? I was young, already a successful journalist, and life in Brighton was buzzing. What should I do with the part of myself that longed for 'something to happen'?

I arrived in Florence almost by accident. Travelling with a friend, we caught the midnight Strasbourg–Firenze Pellegrino. I think there was some kind of romantic involvement in Alsace; I didn't want to leave and Gillian had to push me onto that train.

In a parallel universe, Italy had always been there, waiting for me. When we stood on the Piazza Michelangelo and gazed down onto that city of ochre and terracotta, illuminated by the setting sun, it appeared like one huge palazzo. Magic! I knew there was no turning back, all would now be revealed. With hindsight I realise this was either wishful thinking or the contrived ending of a romantic writer; real life is not like that.

All the same, now I had launched myself onto Italy I could not stop; it became a drug. I was really only happy when on the move. Life in England was an interlude, a time of getting a bit more money together, planning my next journey. Nothing could compare with the excitement of boarding a train in Paris and rushing through the night. The couchette attendant would arrive to pull down the beds and I would lie, sniffing the scent of clean linen, dozing fitfully to be wakened by echoing Kafkaesque voices announcing the mysterious names of stations, or by the random shunting of our train from one track to another.

In the early hours I'd tumble out of bed and go to queue for my turn in the now smelly toilet. My face in the mirror looked ugly and puffy from hours in the confined space of the compartment. It is certainly not the most comfortable way of travelling but I loved it, love it still: that sense of anticipation as the hours pass and you go to stand in the corridor to watch for the long-awaited station to slide into view.

Those trains took me not only further and further south but on a voyage of self-discovery. In retrospect I see such journeying as having a life of its own, springing from a deep need within myself to escape from the bookish young girl, to discover my sensuous self.

'The sun is God,' as the artist J.M.W. Turner is reputed to have said on his deathbed. At that time the sun was *my* god. I pined for it, basked in it; under its benign flame I explored beautiful cities, entered cool museums and galleries; crossed the Lagoon to the island of Murano in a *vaporetto*, climbed towers and gazed over arcaded Bologna. But all the time a part of me remained detached, as if I were watching myself, the heroine of one of those novels I had devoured, to whom something might happen to alter my destiny. However energetically I courted this 'life', in an obscure way I remained in one piece.

Of course there were encounters. I flirted, laughed a lot,

drank wine; met men with mysterious double lives for lunch, never dinner. I woke to the sound of goats and chickens, the Tuscan sun slanting across the bedroom floor with a man named Dante beside me; and in spite of that cautionary tale of Henry James', *Daisy Miller*, I stayed up all night to watch the sun rise in the Forum.

All this until, one late-spring evening, I stood in Rome's Borghese gardens, admiring the famous sunset view from the Pincio Terrace. I watched the sky blaze with light, swallows darting across it like ink drawings in a Japanese picture. Spires and domes seemed to float in the air. My heart lifted as I realised this delightful relationship I'd entered into with Italy could continue indefinitely. Like the swallows etched against the sunset glow, I was free to come and go, to enjoy a bit of *la dolce vita* with no danger of breaking my heart.

Why then did I go to the Press Club? What bad fairy directed me to little Via Mercedes at the hour when foreign correspondents, having filed their day's stories, would be in the bar? I could have strolled through the cooling evening streets, crossed the river to Trastevere, sat at a pavement table in one of the *trattorie* and enjoyed a pizza and some wine. Or I might have joined the evening crowds, had my portrait done by an artist on the Spanish Steps. Like so many life-changing events, it was launched by a random decision. Had I known where it would lead me, I should have turned in the opposite direction, stepped into a phone booth and called my friends, Mario or Antonello. Hindsight, as they say, is a wonderful thing.

I can see myself clearly: I'm sitting at a table in the Press Club bar, my hair cut in a shiny bob, and I'm wearing the pink trouser suit my mother made for me. On the table is a glass of white wine and I'm smoking one of the Italian workmen's cigarettes my boyfriend Dante introduced me to, during my time in Florence. I hear my name called. Glancing towards the bar, I see Leslie. He doesn't have much time, is snatching a beer before he goes out to dinner. I've met him before – I've met the majority of Rome 'stringers'.

Leslie asks me about England but in the vague manner of someone who has cut all ties and become an expat. Naively, I gush about how much I'd like to stay on in Rome; can he put any freelance work my way? In reply, he points to my glass.

'Another?'

Suddenly he seems anxious to get away but, before he leaves, he suggests it: 'Why don't you go down to Sicily? Have a look at Taormina, it's a corner of paradise.'

And that was that.

Two days later, I went to Roma Termini station and bought my ticket. I returned to the hotel, packed my case and carried it down the several flights of stairs. There was no porter; this was a very cheap hotel.

'*Al mare?*' the elderly woman at the reception desk asked me. 'Are you going to the sea?'

I shrugged, the Italian shrug.

What I couldn't tell her because I didn't know myself was the significance of this journey I was about to undertake. It seemed to me just more interminable hours on a train rewarded by the light and joie de vivre of yet another part of Italy.

Not so.

Sicily was my epiphany. It altered me profoundly and I

14

wonder about that change. I had longed to escape England, to travel south, to 'live' like those heroines in the books I read. What I did not bargain for was the conflict of cultures, the infidelity of the Sicilian male who 'does not want to eat spaghetti every day', but who can equally justify it all by adding, 'the wife is the wife, the foreigner is the foreigner.' I was not prepared for Sicily's 'terrifying insularity', as described in Di Lampedusa's *The Leopard*.

I had yearned for romance but I did not reckon on how much innocence one needs to lose in its pursuit, how far the interior journey.

This was the ultimate love affair because it was not so much with a man but a deep and abiding passion for a place. Dangerous when that place is Sicily, mythical island of the monsters Scylla and Charybdis, home of Circe the enchantress; composed of so many elements, blue seas and sky, sun, but also shadows and suffering.

There is not a mountain or a valley that has not run with the blood of invaders. Sicily, gateway to the Mediterranean, North Africa and the Adriatic, has always been a coveted location for trade and colonisation. Here, the Mafia began as a way of life, a means of protecting the family and loved ones from the unjust authority of whatever dominant conqueror was in power. Sicily's oppressive history of many corrupt and judicially inept rulers fostered a mood of self-reliance and respect for family and friends. This history provided the establishment and necessity of the Mafia, an atmosphere where, if you were crafty, you could work the system to your advantage and win wealth, power and status.

When Rome took control of Sicily in 241 BC, the

Romans introduced their feudal system called *latifundia*, large landed estates, which produced grain, olive oil or wine for the benefit of the owner. It was rather like an early form of intensive farming and depended on slave labour. There was also a new justice system where decisions of one area versus another were often very different. The Sicilians, who were used to sustenance farming, growing just enough food to feed themselves and their families, challenged this but Rome upheld the landlords' authority. This social structure of a pecking order paved the way for the Mafia to emerge.

In AD 826, Sicily's next rulers were the Arabs. Although non-Muslims were permitted to practise their own religions, the island came under the influence of Islam. On the positive side, the spread of literature and the arts was encouraged, but, more negatively, it promoted the maltreatment and subordination of women. Later, the Mafia was to adopt this idea and to keep women out of its affairs. Another aspect of Arab law adopted by Sicilians was the idea of internal justice: instead of having a solid system to deal with crime and delinquency, they used personal justice to avenge misdeeds.

Next came the Normans, who annexed Sicily in the eleventh century. Their system reverted back to that of the Romans, of estate managers whose only allegiance was the king. Together with their landlord bosses, they lived by their own rules, creating an even greater inconsistency of justice throughout the island. The Sicilian man in the street took to creating his own small groups and dealing with matters himself rather than going to the authorities. *La Famiglia* was now most important, the unit you could rely on and it has continued so to this day.

16

When the Spanish Aragonese took over power of Sicily in AD 1300, the rulers set a strict limit on information arriving from the outside world; this was almost the reverse of the Arab culture. Sicilians were deprived of the artistic, scientific and agricultural developments arriving with the Italian Renaissance, something that surely made them draw more closely in on themselves. Differences in justice between estates were exacerbated when the Spanish embarked on the Inquisition. By 1487, it was using this to further control the Sicilians. Taxes were lifted for some influential Christians, while others were financially blighted. Signs of unrest were quelled by executions and, as with the Mafia, the Spanish government did a cover-up job. The reaction among the islanders was to turn to internal justice within their group: an early form of Mafia.

Moving on to the nineteenth century, not so very long after the unification of Italy in 1860, power control in a number of the island's small towns concentrated on four elements: the Church, of course; the local aristocrat, who could also be an important landowner, enabled to collect rents but perhaps not taxes; the town hall; and a respected 'gentleman'.

In reality, this gentleman was Mafioso whose army of bully boys would intimidate, extort and even kill. The Mafia, as we know it, was born.

Nevertheless, the question has to be asked of how it is this organisation has survived into the twenty-first century. It is a question of the more things change, the more they remain the same. There continues to exist a lack of confidence in the competence of law enforcement and distrust of the state. Probably the main reason why organised crime continues to be so powerful in the south of Italy is the overall furtiveness of the people, bred out of those centuries of domination. They assume that their politicians are greedy thieves. Businessmen are convinced their associates are poised, ready to steal. Unions expect employees will be exploited; couples take it almost for granted that infidelity is just to be expected. The reaction is not to give anything away, to be crafty and beat the others at their own game.

Looking at Sicily from the outside, many people view the Mafia as the cause of some social problems. In truth, it is the effect, a result of centuries of entrenched customs. There is the *raccomandazioni*, the favouring of one contender over another for personal or expedient reasons, certainly not for those of merit. This colours many facets of Sicilian *modus vivendi*, making it a ripe breeding ground for all forms of corruption, dishonesty and criminality. Then there is nepotism, a 2008 article in the *Economist* reported: 'this week news emerged of a university rector who, the day before he retired on 31 October, signed a decree to make his son a lecturer. At Palermo University, as many as 230 teachers are reported to be related to other teachers'. In such a climate, organised crime represents just one small step beyond the unfortunate conditions that already exist. Sicilian politicians literally buy votes with promises of employment or other gifts.

THREE

In the Shadow of Etna

I knew nothing of this background that first morning, that first arrival after the journey travelling the length of Calabria, its interminable bays, sitting upright for hours, my companion a tiny Sicilian woman offering *panini* stuffed with salami and pungent cheese, black bitter coffee from a flask.

As we crossed the straits of Messina and I stood on the ferry deck, the light changed from grey to purple, then purple to rose and the tip of the sun flamed over the sea. I looked out at deserted beaches where gold-tipped waves broke over the shore. The air was warm at five in the morning. We must have stopped at a dozen stations, each seemed identical with curly thirties' lettering and potted oleanders.

Suddenly, Taormina − the station locked in an exquisite time warp, a ceiling of carved panels and Victorian ironwork on the ticket booths.

In a bar filled with the scent of coffee and strong tobacco I ordered a *cappuccino*. This was a world where things '*happened*', I told myself: '*Now I begin to live.*'

And then that drive up to Taormina, the serpentine roads and villas crouched behind blowsy shrubs, palm trees. And always that glimpse of blue sky and Etna's plume of smoke on the still air. I did not see any shadows, not until much later.

When something so profound happens, what do you do? Avoid. Stay home or travel to other places; but all the same, and especially if you venture once more into Italy, it is inevitable you will hear the siren call. Which, if you are sensible, you will ignore. Until that moment when, like the bird whose nest is plundered but returns and returns, you experience a desire to create a meaning out of loss.

And that is what I did.

When the offer of a 'small apartment looking over the sea' came up, I decided to take it for six weeks and embark on the 'Sicilian' book I had long planned.

I did not reckon on the advent of Lizzie.

FOUR

Syracuse — A Sicilian Farewell

We had taken a day off to escape to Syracuse, choosing it as the one Sicilian city Andrew shouldn't miss. It was a painful decision. Should we leave Lizzie all day? we pondered. Was there a possibility she could get out of the apartment? Would she be all right?

But Andrew's ten-day stay in Taormina was passing and we'd hardly done anything. He'd been very good about all the changes of plan, spending afternoons at the table on the lower terrace with a book and cans of beer. Admittedly, it wasn't much of a sacrifice, with that incomparable view over the bay of Isola Bella. We'd done some local things, sat in the shade of the town's splendid public gardens, taken the bus along the coast. It hadn't helped that this spring had been disappointing, unlike the Sicilian springs I remembered from years ago. When we tried to swim, the sea was icy.

Lizzie had taken no notice of us. She suffered her imprisonment in silence under the bed, though managing to scoff the tasty morsels we put down for her; but we hadn't felt we could leave her alone for a whole day until now.

Syracuse lay prostrate under the sun: filled with tourists, each wearing a shady hat. We trailed behind them along the crowded Via Cavour, making for the narrow lanes of the old part of the city, Ortygia Island. It is a lovely place, the light clear and blue, evoking a definite sense of Greece. The sun glared down. Ironic that on the first really hot day we'd left the beach behind.

It was a relief to reach the Marina and step under the ficus trees, which line this waterside promenade. And so we arrived at Piazza Duomo. But it was lunchtime and the cathedral was closed so we would have to content ourselves with the guidebook.

There was a book called *A Cypress in Sicily*, which I used to read over and over again when I lived in Taormina. Author Howard Agg described Syracuse as the one-time New York of the ancient world, the thriving metropolis of Magna Graecia. It once rivalled Athens as the largest and most beautiful city in Greek times. I found it a labyrinth of intricately paved streets that open up into squares: an expansive, vital place unlike many other Sicilian cities, with their narrow roads and pocket-sized piazzas. Ortygia is connected to the mainland by several bridges and ringed by ancient city walls, relics of the defences designed by Archimedes. Considering it is a modern city, the sense remains of continuity from the period of antiquity and the mythological themes dominating that epoch: temples, castles, fountains, amphitheatres, piazzas and palazzos, all awash with the light and air of the surrounding sea.

The present cathedral stands on layers of pagan temples. It is an example of the sacred/profane aspect of Sicily, where pictures of the Virgin Mary stand cheek by jowl with rings to ward off the Evil Eye. Religious *festas* may start off with the parade of an effigy — Saint Pancrazio, patron saint of Taormina, for example — but the day finishes up in carousing.

We stared at the front of the cathedral and tried to imagine what it must have looked like as the Doric Temple of Athena: magnificent, stuffed with art treasures, the golden shield of the warring goddess reflecting the sun's rays. I had an even stronger sense of the past, of violation and blood, as we stood before the Altar of Hieron 11, where the guidebook told us 450 bulls were sacrificed to Zeus in a day.

While Andrew went to order beers, I sat at a cafe table and thought of feral Lizzie. What a relief it was to have escaped for a day. I hadn't realised how difficult it would be to keep her closed up in the apartment. She had soon released herself from the Elizabethan collar Giulio had put on her; all she wanted was to be out roaming free.

I don't think any cat is wholly domesticated. One interesting thing I've learned in my ongoing dialogue with my cat Sheba is that cats lead a double life. In the house she is an overgrown kitten, gazing up at her human owners. Out on the tiles she's her own boss, a free-living wild creature. The moment a cat manages to persuade a human being to open a door she is off and away without a backward glance. While a dog might look back to see if the human pack mate is following, not so the cat. Her mind has floated off into a totally feline world, where two-legged creatures don't exist. Cats have the dual capacity to evolve and revert to atavistic principles. In Lizzie's case she had never known a home, a warm hearth, and food put in front of her. Her life was spent in watchful survival. Was it any wonder she considered me her captor?

I glanced at my watch; I had an image of Lizzie and felt anxious: should we go back?

It had been comparatively easy to get to Syracuse but, as so often happens in Sicily, it turned out to be much more difficult to return. There was a two-and-a-half-hour wait for the next train. We resigned ourselves and went to sit in the station cafe. I drank a cheap but good red wine at a few liras a glass, while Andrew had a beer. It was obviously the local bar. At a neighbouring table a group of men played cards. Every now and then one of them shouted out 'Scopa!' It took me back to winter evenings in Taormina's Arco Rosso bar.

I'd sit in a corner, nursing a glass of wine. I'd watch the groups of men crouched over cards fancifully designed as knights on horseback, swords and daggers, goblets, sheaves of corn and golden coins: the Sicilian game Briscola. Hawkish eyes would follow every card as it was thumped down until someone shouted 'Scopa!'

Sitting in that bar, I used to wonder what on earth I was doing there. A vision of Brighton would rush into my mind, the flags flying straight out in the breeze that never really drops, my mother waiting alone in the seafront flat. After a few months I had to go home to see her; the cord between us was never truly broken.

Just as we were getting quite merry on the local brew,

we realised our train had arrived while we'd begun to enjoy ourselves in this shabby little station cafe. Sicily is like that. Within hours you can begin to imagine yourself thinking: *OK, we'll stop here and find a pensione.* If you did stay, I would bet that within days you'd enter into the *domani domani* mentality. D.H. Lawrence was right, the South does cure you of caring.

It was one of the dreaded *locale* trains, which scarcely get up speed before they start to slow down for the next station. They're pretty stations hung with baskets of trailing geraniums, but there are far too many of them.

About fifteen minutes out of Syracuse, a young man got on; he wore the latest in designer jeans and an Inter-Milan sports shirt, an Italian computer magazine tucked under his arm. At first sight I'd put him down as one of a new breed, which had broken the habit of living at home until the age of forty. This was an Italian man who'd struck out on his own. Then I noticed the bulging plastic bags he deposited gently on the seat. Ah! I knew those bags. I'd come across them on many a journey in Italy: cornucopias of food, every type of delicacy, from chicken fragrant with rosemary, pots of aubergines and tomatoes *sott'olio*, whole cheeses and salami. They represented *La Mamma*'s obsessive fear that her child might face famine during the journey, or not find the quality food he was accustomed to.

The young man made himself comfortable and opened his magazine. We settled back with our books.

'Soon be home,' Andrew said. 'Shall we eat out tonight?'

But the train didn't move. Another five minutes and it remained stationary, not a whistle for departure, not a judder… nothing. Giovanni or Stefano, or whatever his name might be was not about to be whisked away from his Sicilian homeland. He began to read but I could see he was losing his concentration; he didn't appear so cocky. As he looked across he met my eye. We shrugged. Another few minutes and he dived into one of the plastic bags and pulled out a *panino*. And what a *panino*! It bristled with nourishment: mozzarella and ham, tomato and olives. He bit hugely and olive oil trickled through his fingers. I could imagine the authority of its preparation. His father might have been dithering about, clapping his son on the shoulder, saying it was good to see him and not to make it so long before he came home again, but it was only thanks to *La Mamma* the household ran like clockwork. Early-morning calls would be organised, coffee made ready and those plastic bags stacked with food against likely starvation. Men may run Italy but it is the women who run men. When I thought about it, everything made sense. What do Italians call out in times of distress? *Mamma Mia*!

The mystery of the becalmed train was now revealed: we had been waiting for somebody. Here she came, a slender young woman in jeans appearing at the end of the platform, a young man behind her, struggling with two large suitcases. The retinue that followed made a great deal of noise and I prayed they wouldn't choose our carriage but they did, halting outside our window, laughing and talking and giving the girl advice. 'Be good, phone this evening', 'Take care' and the ubiquitous '*Ciao*!' Our companion glanced up, gave an audible sigh and went back to his magazine. I was fascinated by this group: there was a strong-featured woman in a two-piece, whose thick legs ended in court shoes, a tall, thin man with wonderful mustachios, and a little man with a weasel face, wearing a trilby. There was also a much younger woman, jiggling a fat baby, and a boy in a T-shirt and shorts, trying to restrain a dog with floppy ears and a long muzzle. The young woman kissed them all on both cheeks but she wouldn't get away as easily as that.

And here they came: the supplies against the famine she was about to face when she started travelling North. At last she was seated with her two cases stowed above our heads. She glanced round at us, resembling a pretty pussycat with large brown eyes. Andrew and I glared back: her enormous family had no right to hold up a train. But now, as it drew away, they pressed forward and presented themselves with every accessory and behaviour as though taking part in a sentimental Victorian scene, 'The Farewell'. They shouted, wept and waved handkerchiefs; the dog just wagged his tail.

Andrew and I had been treated to another sighting of 'The Family' sticking together out of blind instinct, fearful of ever being alone. The Italy of the family is the quintessential Italy. Of course there are feuds; there are even, in Sicily, members of the same family skulking behind prickly pears with rifles, waiting to kill one another. But as a rule the family is the family and it revolves around children — everything is done for the *bambini*. Their smallest wish must be granted. Italians love children. A crowd will gather round a pretty baby just to admire such a wonderful object.

I'd had my own experience with the Italian family and its less positive features when I first came to Sicily and fell in love with a Sicilian. Amadeo and I got on swimmingly, laughing, loving, and generally being young and in love. All went well until *La Famiglia* descended for the obligatory August holiday. They expected I would spend all my time with them and could not understand my need for silence and space to read and write. Every single day they shopped at the market and cooked enormous lunches and dinners. Once, when Amadeo's brother was called away for a day on business, his return was reminiscent of the Prodigal Son, complete with feasting until dawn. Like cuckoos, they finally usurped my nest and thrust me out into the cold.

On the train, the young woman opened a magazine and settled down. She was going away, but you knew she would return.

Sicilians travel the world but Circe's island always calls them back.

FIVE

The Secret Lives of Feral Cats

I kept Lizzie captive for almost three weeks while her leg mended until she was at last ready to be released. Looking back, I marvel how I did it and whether I was completely mad. She was my first experience of feral cats and I had no notion of their lifestyle. As a child, there had always been cats and kittens in our household – my father in particular was a feline fan. Tabitha, Mrs White Puss, Ginger and Biscuit… they were purring, friendly creatures who loved to be stroked and petted. They liked to play and to snuggle up on any available lap.

Feral cats are as wild as their ancestors and like any other wild creature they have an innate mistrust of human beings. The mother cats take a firm paw with their kittens, training them to be quiet and stay put. A meow might attract predators, as could the movement of kittens running about and playing. Often a feral cat that is taken into a home or shelter will revert to a playful kitten, making up for its childhood. Mothers will also make their kittens wash and wash to remove the scent of food from their fur, which again could attract the enemy. Their games have grim undertones preparing the offspring for the life of a feral. A mother may play very roughly with the dominant male kitten, training him to be an alpha male. She will teach her kittens to go to the food dish, forever watchful and poised to run, should a human appear. It is a game, but one of survival.

Dogs like wide, open spaces; cats like security. The mothers make their kittens follow them in a row like ducklings, and discipline those who get out of line, another survival instinct. They allow play at dawn and dusk when the night predators are not around but it is light enough for them to see well, but they make their kittens go into a safe place at night.

Many of them have spent their entire existence living rough near a source of food: a waste heap, dustbin or in the vicinity of a hotel or restaurant. Their lives are based on scrounging for scraps of food, often very scarce, and reproducing. They are likely to be riddled with fleas or ticks and certainly have worms. The tomcat battles for supremacy and can inflict nasty wounds on the female in their savage mating.

A human cat bond can be forged if the feral kitten is handled early enough in its life. Even so, not all kittens are the same and their degree of friendliness depends on other factors, such as the father's genes. Also, because the female will have mated with several toms there can be different temperaments within the same litter of kittens as well as different colourings. The older they become, the more difficult it is to alter their wild nature, as I found with Lizzie.

When we opened that trap in Giulio's surgery, I had no idea what I was about to take on. Lizzie's one thought was to escape – throwing herself against the walls, dashing round the room; anything to get away from us. During her time in the apartment she was constantly stressed, wanting to be outdoors leading the life she knew. Anyone who takes it upon herself to tame a feral feline is in for a long haul. Humans have to learn to think like a feral and never to force contact: touching is viewed as a threat and direct eye contact regarded as aggression. If she is frightened she is likely to attack, and feral cat scratches can be very nasty indeed. As time passed and I gained experience in working with feral cats, I came to realise that the best way to help them is to catch them and have them neutered before returning them to their colony. It might seem a brutal existence to us, but it is usually far more unkind to take them away.

A few days later, I was in the bus park seeing Andrew onto the airport bus, bound for England. I waved him goodbye and shed a few tears. This had been an extraordinary time together. Then I went back to the apartment and Lizzie. Now I was alone and free to enjoy my contemplation of Isola Bella.

Every time I left the apartment, my little tower, I noticed a group of people standing on the nearby Belvedere gazing down at The View. I photographed it at different times of the day: morning, noon, evening, it was never the same. Fluctuating with the mood of the weather, it seemed to have a persona of its own; I had become enchanted by this constantly changing scene.

The light changed all the time and the blue through

shades of cerulean to turquoise to jade. Sometimes the water resembled ribbed silk as the currents from the Messina straits streamed in. Other times the sun painted it with molten silver so dazzling you needed dark glasses to gaze at it.

I never grew tired of looking.

SIX

The Cats of the Public Gardens

I was sitting in Taormina's Public Gardens talking to the cats. The gardens house a colony of feral felines, which grows or diminishes depending on the number of animals abandoned and whether someone throws down poisoned meatballs. A lot of Sicilians look upon ferals as vermin.

Lily was sitting on my lap, her eyes narrowed to slits as I gently scratched under her chin, a favourite place for cats, though each is different. I thought that she must be over eight years old and, unlike some of her companions who ran away, she had worked out it was politic to allow stroking because then she would get the lion's share of any titbits.

The afternoon was so hot it seemed to be holding its breath; time was suspended. I'd chosen to come here and sit in this green shade rather than bake on the beach of Isola Bella, hundreds of metres below the town. I couldn't face being squashed into a bus packed with people – all that tourist panic of where or where not to get off.

As I stroked Lily, I gazed at a truly picture postcard view: huge pots overflowing with geraniums, pink and red, standing on a stone parapet, and further beyond grumpy Etna rising against the perfectly blue sky.

Lily purred. It wouldn't be hard to nod off myself.

'*Sera*.' Rounding a flowerbed, the familiar figure of Maria arrived, out of breath, carrying two large plastic bags.

'*Sera*, Maria.'

She and I had met here too often to stand on ceremony. Besides, it was too hot.

She set the bags down, gathered up the feeding bowls and gave them a rinse in the fountain. Immediately the cats sprang into action. Lily's eyes widened and she flew from my lap. The air was filled with meows. The cats milled round Maria, pressing themselves against her legs as she emptied out great mounds of pasta cooked with fish. Then there was a lot of grumbling, a lashing out of paws as they fought for their place. They were a pretty sad bunch, but even when they are starving cats retain their table manners – about twenty of them, ginger, black and tortoiseshell; the big grey tom had a weeping raw patch behind his ear, several were thin and mangy and there was a small white cat with one eye. I knew how he lost that: a vicious infection akin to feline chlamydia, which is actually part of a feline upper respiratory disease complex, most often appears in cats as conjunctivitis, which is inflammation of the tissues of the eye, also known as 'pink eye'.

Unless it is treated in time with an antibiotic like Pensulvit cream, the animal loses its sight. I carried a tube of this cream in my bag but it really needed two people on the job: one to hold the cat, the other to spread the cream. The two sickly ginger kittens I noticed the other day were absent. Theirs is a grim world.

Maria plumped herself down on the bench beside me and began to speak in the Sicilian dialect. She did this in the understandable belief that, because we shared a love of cats and the desire to help them, I should be able to understand her. In a way, I suppose I did, at least the gist of what she said. It's a language packed with guttural sounds and with only a nodding acquaintance with Italian. Pronunciation is easier for a Brit because the 'r' isn't emphatically rolled. At Maria's age she was no longer jealous of foreign females, thank goodness! Often I'd been the subject of a penetrating glare when I tried to befriend other Sicilian women.

She was beautiful, not outwardly, I should add. Elderly, with a strong-featured face and grey hair, she wore the typical matron's dark frock. Her varicose veins gave her trouble, she'd often told me about them: '*Mi fanno morire nel caldo*' (they kill me in the hot weather). Without grace, she sat with her legs splayed, showing her knee-highs. But Maria was beautiful within. She had a generous, loving heart, a childlike simplicity. The several badges of animal welfare associations she wore on her collar announced her devotion. She was a widow and had moved from a house into an apartment so she couldn't keep cats of her own. But every day – whatever the season – she bought fish from the market, cooked it up with pasta and brought it here.

She related the trouble she was having with her neighbours, who were suspicious of her strange behaviour; this is a society where anything new or unusual is mistrusted and her eccentric feeding of cats was not tolerated. As she described the nasty tricks they played on her, like watering their plants just after she had hung out her washing on the balcony below, I gazed round the gardens.

Nearby were some gigantic terracotta pots filled with cascading plants covered with tiny scarlet bells; the label said they came from Mexico. The roses were already in bloom and the bougainvilleas as I always remembered them: gaudy and riotous, a clash of magenta and crimson.

'I worry – I really worry what would happen to these *bambini* if I couldn't get here anymore. Sometimes I've been ill and missed a few days. I've lain in my bed imagining them waiting here for me and I don't come,' Maria told me.

SEVEN

Some Encounters with Cat Ladies

Maria's voice brought me back to myself. She stroked a grey and white cat with blue eyes, surely a touch of the Siamese there and probably abandoned when the novelty of kittenish behaviour wore off.

Maria was a *gattara*, a woman who feeds cats.

Occasionally I have seen elderly men standing in piazzas or among ancient ruins dishing out food from Whiskas tins but usually the *gattare* are women. Some people joke about them, sneering that the creatures are a child substitute. But they don't recognise the heroic dedication of the often-elderly woman, dragging her basket on wheels, heavy with cat food towards 'her' colony. In Rome, it is these cat ladies who care for many of the estimated 180,000 stray cats prowling the city's streets. One of the most famous was the beautiful actress Anna Magnani, who used to feed the cats at Torre Argentina every day when she was appearing in the nearby theatre. In the UK, former supermodel Celia Hammond, whose face once graced the cover of *Vogue* magazine during the 1960s, is a dedicated *gattara*. For decades she has been rescuing, neutering and re-homing stray and unwanted animals.

'It's very hard to do this job and have a normal life,' she has been quoted as saying. 'Relationships just fall apart, I've had three main ones and I neglected all of them, which is why I'm on my own.'

She sometimes ends up working twenty-two hours a day helping cats and says her modelling days feel so far removed from her life now. It is as though they happened to a different person.

'You only get one life, you have to do what you feel is right with it. If you have a lifestyle where you have spent your whole existence taking drugs, going to parties, flying all over the world and lying on the beach, what would you feel at the end of your life?'

Maria's fear of letting the cats down is common among these women. Their lives are composed of considerable sacrifices and small gratification. As one of them told me: 'I've sold everything, my rings, my gold, everything but I can't abandon them.' She had been feeding cats for twenty years.

I wanted to put my arm round my companion, she looked so sad and alone sitting there, but then Lily pushed herself against Maria's leg. She never missed the chance of a lap to make herself comfortable on.

In a while, Maria heaved herself to her feet, rinsed the bowls that had been licked clean anyway, and filled one with water. She gave me one of her rare smiles. '*A domani*,' she said and trundled off. I could see her legs were troubling her this sultry afternoon.

As I wandered along the paths, gazing at flowers, I recognised some of them: hibiscus, oleander, African marigolds, but others were unknown to me. *You've changed*, I told myself. *Fifteen years ago, you'd have loved the colours and the perfumes of this garden but more likely you'd have been thinking about the latest amore you were meeting that evening. You certainly wouldn't have got all these cats' hairs over your white trousers!*

She was like a stranger, that other Jenny. Did she ever notice that each of the old olive trees lining the last path towards the exit gate bears a plaque commemorating a soldier fallen in the First World War? Did she bother to find out that the nickname for those strange askew wooden pavilions is 'the beehives'? I don't think she did. In the gap between my visits I'd changed and Taormina hadn't – only it seemed different to me because my viewpoint was new.

I arrive at the bust of Florence Trevelyan in a little enclosure. Her hair is drawn back into a bun and she wears a locket on her high-necked blouse; she's smiling a secret little smile. Florence, daughter of Lord Edward Spencer. Born in Newcastle in 1852, Queen Victoria called her 'my little niece'. Photographs of the period show her among flowers and dogs in the royal parks. No one knows exactly what happened to Florence until she was twenty-seven years old. It was then in April 1879 that she left England to travel for more than two years. She doesn't seem to have been very enthusiastic about this; rather than a pleasure trip, it seems she was going away to forget a love affair rumoured to be with Victoria's son Edward.

She and her travelling companion, Louise Harriet Perceval, arrived in Italy, where they visited all the big cities. Florence was an avid diary writer. Arriving in Messina in a February of the early 1880s, she noted 'nothing worth the trouble of visiting' and promptly left by train for Taormina. This was a different story altogether, as she wrote to her 'dear cousin'.

The journey from Taormina railway station was 'marvellous, great, stupendous, immense, very picturesque, beautiful, seductive with the view of Etna. The sea is blue and the mountains: it is impossible to describe how beautiful they are.'

Like many other visitors, she finally felt at home in Taormina and it was a regretful departure. On her return to England in August 1881, life apparently ceased to be a fairy story. Something serious happened between Lady Trevelyan and the Royal family. Dino Papale, author of *Taormina Segreta*, suggests that in 1884 she once more departed England, leaving everything behind 'as if she were running away' and journeyed to Taormina.

It is said that Queen Victoria had 'invited' her to travel abroad for a lengthy period in order to try to make her forget Edward. But on her return and with the renewed interest of her son, Her Majesty appears to have decided there was nothing for it but to exile Florence for twenty years.

Florence arrived in Sicily one February and six years later became engaged to Professor Salvatore Cacciola. The couple met when Florence banged on the door of his villa, demanding he treat her terrier. 'I'm a doctor, not a vet!' he protested. Nevertheless, he not only cured the dog but also married its owner.

Florence turned her back on the past and threw herself into life in Taormina, created these gardens and built little pavilions where she could take afternoon tea. When she died in October 1907 , she left her gardens to her beloved husband on the condition that 'the trees must not be cut down and no houses built. All the creatures of whatever kind: dogs, cats, parrots, raven, doves, tortoises, canaries and other birds must be looked after with loving care as I did in my life'.

You're a lady after my own heart, Florence, I thought.

I photographed six black kittens playing near the entrance to the gardens, oblivious to the cars, which swing round from Via Roma. Then I spotted some other flowers with huge obscene stamens luring the bees. In spite of water problems, Sicily is greener and lusher than its neighbours in the Mediterranean. There is an astonishing fecundity of swift blossoming and fruitfulness, which as quickly fades. This reminded me of the love affairs in the town, of the spoilt-for-choice attitude of the men who select women from the coaches that arrive and depart each week from Catania airport.

If I've learned anything about life, it is change is the only constant thing and love so often transitory, not the 'happy ever after' I used to believe. I could not imagine I could become again the Jenny who turned her back on everything and gave herself up to the sun, the girl who found everything 'lovely' but whose eyes failed to see the plaques on the olive trees. Could I fall in love with another Sicilian man? It was hard to imagine.

Opposite a ceramic shop there is a series of steps leading down to a narrow street. Motorbikes and cars rush past, yet against a garage door are set a series of bowls, a sure sign of *gattara* territory. This colony is more nervous than that of the gardens. Tourists don't come here as a rule. As I approached, they ran across the road almost under the wheels of a motorbike and peered out at me warily through some railings. After a while a small woman approached: it was Gabriella.

She resembled a bag lady. Her broken sandals tied to her feet over thick stockings, she wore an old dress and what looked like several cardigans over the top. But it was her face that always held my attention: it was rather round, with a small chin and wide-set eyes. She must have been a beauty when she was young but now that skin was sallow and leathery. And she smelled musty – unwashed – an overpowering stink!

When I mentioned this to a friend who lived nearby, he laughed and said, 'You mean *La Baronessa*. Oh yes, I know her! When she comes into the bank, we all make sure we stand upwind. She smells ten times worse when it's been raining.'

It was an appalling stench but I stood my ground while we talked, this time in Italian, about the cats. She told me once again how she spent all her pension money on them and, although in bad health, she still came down here every day.

Then she launched into the story everyone has heard ad nauseam: how she was born in Milan, married a Taorminese and came here when she was very young. How the family ran a restaurant at Isola Bella. They were happy days, such happy days all that time ago. Now she was over eighty and some days she didn't know how she got herself down here. But if she didn't, who would? I watched as she doled out the food, talking softly to another raggedy little group. *I couldn't end up like her, could I?*

Later, I called at the butcher, averting my gaze from the sight of the skinned rabbits, looking horribly human, hanging overhead. Instead, I watched the red worms of beef exuding from the mincer. Everything is spotless and absolutely fresh in Sicilian butchers' shops. Even I, a vegetarian, had to admit that. When I arrived back at my apartment I'd cook the meat slowly, then add lentils and rice to give it bulk. Tomorrow I'd take it to the Public Gardens.

And I asked myself: *Was I to become like Florence Trevelyan, a strange Englishwoman who reinvented herself and found fulfilment in helping animals?* Whether I liked it or not, the fact was, I was fast becoming a *gattara*.

EIGHT

An Appointment with Taormina

As the week went by, I was feeling the strain of having a feral cat in the apartment. I missed Andrew's down-to-earth approach, although we spoke nightly on the phone. There was the daily chore of cleaning out her litter tray and trips to the butcher for mince, which she seemed to thoroughly enjoy. It must have been a welcome change to her normal diet of scraps. She had become less timid of me and came out from under the bed when I was around. But if I made any move to touch her, she darted away – her mother had trained her well.

My stay in Taormina was turning out to be very different from the one I'd planned: the excursions, the interviews for my long-imagined book, all must be abandoned now because of this small feline. But I only had to remember that image of Lizzie with her terrible injury to be content with what I was doing.

One morning, I decided to walk through the backstreets of this little town. Away from the Corso and its nightly street theatre, you step into the world of day-to-day life. In Via Numitorio, a caged bird sang its heart out. I paused to read some of those wry ceramic plaques showing the Sicilian biting sense of humour and pleasure in philosophising. One I knew: 'A guest is like a fish –after three days he stinks'. Others were less familiar: 'The viper that bit my mother-in-law died – poisoned' and even: 'Eat well, excrete well and you needn't be afraid of death'. Some builders sang a Sicilian melody as they worked on a new house in Via Giardinazzo.

I stopped at Auteri, the ironmonger-cum-everything else shop that never failed me, no matter what I needed, from glue to a toilet plunger. The two elderly owners gaze at the customer over their glasses and then rummage and produce exactly what she is looking for. I could never fathom how they remembered where it might be among all those boxes and shelves of their cavernous store.

I went up and down flights of steps, up and down. Taormina is not for the lazy walker, if you truly want to know it. In a backstreet I paused outside the kitchen of Cyclopes and heard a chef singing. I sniffed the delicious scent of fish being cooked in the simple way: *San Moriglio*, with parsley, garlic, lemon and oil. A little open-backed van skimmed along, loaded with fennel and red onions.

This might have been Taormina before the tourists invaded. I wished I could have seen it. But beautiful as it is, you still wonder how it has reached these heights of popularity; in August you can scarcely make your way along the Corso. One significant event in its tourist history was the chance visit of a young German painter to what was then a practically unknown Sicilian village.

When Otto von Geleng set out from Rome to visit Sicily in 1859, there would have been no road linking the village to the coast. His journey through the precipitous ravines from Giardini was on the back of a mule. He stayed in Taormina for two or three months and it must have made a great impression on him because two years later he returned. Soon he was courting the sister of a Sicilian baron; he married her and settled in the town. The natural beauty of the place inspired him and before long he had painted enough oils and watercolours to hold an exhibition in Paris. Scenes of Taorminese gardens aflame with tropical flowers in brilliant sunlight while Etna glittered with snow, painted in the winter months, astonished visitors, who could not believe such a climate existed in Europe. Geleng was surely making it up!

As a kind of wager, Geleng invited three of his most sceptical critics to come and see for themselves this fishing village situated between Catania and Messina. If they did not find it was exactly as he had depicted, he would foot the bill. He knew he was on a safe wicket for, of course, he had not exaggerated. They were enchanted by the exotic colours and beautiful views and wrote back to friends in France until articles about Geleng's Taormina began to appear in newspapers. In the Place du Tertre, Montmartre, all they could talk about was this unknown fishing village suspended between a turquoise sea and sky, with a smoking volcano, while at the same time there were almond trees in blossom, oranges, lemons and cactuses. Soon Geleng realised that Taormina could flourish if more visitors were encouraged but the town would have to smarten itself up; there was room for a lot of improvement.

Involving himself in local affairs, he emphasised that, if the foreigner was to undertake the necessarily long journey, he must find decent accommodation and at least some of the amenities he was accustomed to in his own country. At that time there was no hotel or inn in the place, no light or running water, only stone cisterns for collecting rain. Refuse was thrown into the streets and conditions were rather primitive. But Geleng's forceful personality persuaded the Taorminese to put their house in order. A hotel, the Timeo, was opened in 1873 with a few rooms (later to be enlarged by the redoubtable Florence Trevelyan). The streets were cleaned, running water was introduced and no longer did the tourist have to grope his way through darkened streets at night.

At one o'clock all the shutters in Taormina clang down and everyone goes for lunch, but I wasn't hungry. I took a left turn and walked down the steps to the old Naumachia, a monumental Roman supporting wall in brick, some 122 metres long, punctuated by huge niches. The name 'Naumachia' literally translates as 'naval battles'. In fact, at one time it was believed that the monument was an aquatic circus representing such battles. In reality, it was a huge aqua theatre, a colossal fountain playing water.

I remembered it as a dank, insalubrious place but now I saw it had been cleaned up and planted with flowers. A notice said it was the work of the local gardeners group.

I admired the lilies, roses and marigolds, then caught sight of a black man crouched by the door of the Arcate restaurant, devouring spaghetti with a dab of tomato sauce. The Taorminese have tender hearts: if they have never been hungry, race memory recalls those who suffered under Sicily's conquerors. Tender but also passionate, their tempers are easily provoked. Quarrels can break out, insults hurled that would sever an English friendship for life, but not here. You will see the combatants next day strolling along the Corso, arm in arm. They have not forgotten the incident but they do not intend it to create an eternal rift. The Taorminese knows when the moment has come to draw in his horns. He does not commit himself to anything, not even an appointment, always allowing a loophole for escape. It's foolish to make a man an enemy, he reasons, you might need him tomorrow or the day after.

I hesitated, wondering whether to go inside the Arcate. I had a dim recollection of the last time I saw Turri; that I did not part on very good terms with this sometime acquaintance.

The restaurant was empty. From the kitchen I heard the sound of clattering pans, sniffed the unmistakable scents of Sicilian cooking – the garlic, the basil, the *pesce spada*. I cleared my throat. Turri, an incorrigible Taormina 'character', appeared in the doorway, an apron tied round his waist. He stared.

'Good heavens, *you*!' was all he said. But he seemed pleased to see me. 'I've just got to finish what I'm doing. Go up to the terrace and I'll be with you in a minute.'

Beyond the flight of steps was a delightful area gazing out over the rooftops. I could see the care that had gone into creating it – the white awning overhead, fresh flowers on the tables, pretty linen – but it was deserted.

'I know.' Turri nodded, pouring wine from the jug into our glasses. 'I don't know what to do. It's the kind of people who come on holiday, these days.'

'I'm surprised they don't want to come to a lovely little place like this.'

'Things aren't what they were. People don't go in for proper lunch, these days. They'll buy a slice or two of pizza or a burger and then go and sit in the Irish pub.'

'But you can't hear yourself speak,' I added, thinking of another pub I had sat in briefly the other day but had to leave, unable to write or think because of the constant loud music.

'Do you really need pubs here?' I asked.

'*Muh!*'

For a moment we sipped our wine and looked back on the Taormina of all those years ago.

'Not married then?' Turri demanded.

I pondered aloud on why my romantic dreams have never been realised. How all these years I have come and gone, increasingly drawn to the little town but I have never found anyone who matches my romantic image.

Turri charged me with this: 'Romantics are always sad. You should forget about romanticism, get on with life!' And then: 'Are you going to have something to eat?'

I ordered *arrabbiata*, angry pasta – it went with my mood.

While I waited, I thought about what he'd said. I mused that, whatever foreign women believe, the Italians are practical, earthy people, aware that life is fleeting. I remembered my first Sicilian love Amadeo's favourite saying: take life as it comes. And if you retort that life is difficult, always ready to rise up and smack you on the nose, they refuse to know about remorse or recriminations.

If it's OK, it's OK, why think about tomorrow? No problem! And if you mention surely actions may have repercussions and responsibilities, how can one live in this fatalistic way, '*Muh!*' they shrug.

Turri came back, set the plate in front of me and refilled my glass. A group of people had appeared and they were sitting round a large table consuming large quantities of wine. Turri's attention wandered; like mothers, restaurateurs, it seems, have a super sensibility to desires even before they are expressed.

'So you're here for good now?' I asked.

'Yes, I suppose so.'

'Don't you miss the cruise ships?'

'I had a good life,' he grinned. 'Girl in every port, but home is home.'

I thought of that song, '*La Terra Amara*' (The Bitter Earth). Many Sicilian villages are abandoned because the young don't want to work on the land anymore. They've left for the cities. And yet, as Turri confirmed, there is this pull to return.

'What about your wife?'

He shrugged.

I remembered the dissatisfied woman who disliked anything that was not Irish. Marriage has made a cynic of Turri. Though they are often criticised, it is not always the fault of these men. There are foreign women who arrive in the town with only one idea in mind: to have a good time, to be wined and dined and to pay for it with their bodies. Many a young Taorminese in search of his *inamorata* has been met with: 'Who are you? What are you doing here? It was just a holiday romance!'

Turri's marriage was over; he accepted it philosophically, almost passively. Meanwhile, the day was to be enjoyed. *Follow your instincts, feelings may develop or not…*

There was something in me that still didn't want to hear this. I, with my romantic temperament bred out of misty castles and ghostly visitations, could not accept this very present view. On the other hand, they were probably right. That way you cannot be disenchanted because you never had any romantic illusions in the first place. Perhaps it is in their genes, a part of their past; their passive waiting for yet another culture to dominate them, an innate self-preservation.

Take life as it comes… I wish I could.

NINE

Goodbye
Lizzie

I finally called Giulio and asked him to come and give Lizzie a check-up. Her leg was now well in place and we agreed it was time for her to return to her colony in Castelmola. The problem was how to get her into a carrying basket; she had no notion that we were trying to help her and retreated to her usual hiding place under the bed. We were forced to poke her out with a stick. At this she went wild, dashing from cover to cover and finally throwing herself against the open window, almost breaking the mosquito netting. At any moment she would be through and there was nothing to stop her falling many feet onto the garden below. Fortunately, Giulio clad in those strong gauntlets managed to grab her and unceremoniously stuff her into the basket.

As the car wound up the now familiar steep roads to the little village, I gazed out of the car window with a sense of nostalgia. I looked back to that day Andrew and I had discovered Lizzie and the weeks that followed, sharing her recovery. I'd become attached to my little waif and now I had to let go. My stay in Taormina was almost at an end; once I had deposited this small cat, only a few days remained before I returned to England. I felt altered by the experience, already beginning to view Sicily with a different eye.

We found her street without difficulty this time and, setting the basket on the place where Andrew and I first saw her, opened the door and stepped back. Lizzie shot out, hesitated for a moment and then dashed away.

'Not even a thank you,' I said.

'You don't need one,' Giulio remarked. 'Look what you've done for her. Shall we go?'

But I felt I couldn't leave it at that: I told him I would stay there in Castelmola for a while and return by bus. We shook hands.

'Thank you.'

He gave me his amused smile. 'It was a pleasure, Jenny. Call me the next time you are in Taormina.'

I watched him go, swinging the basket. There was no sign of Lizzie. Giulio was right: I'd completed my mission and she was back where she belonged. Maybe I'd go back to Taormina and have a few hours on the beach. Behind me, a door opened and a slender woman wearing a flowery pinafore stood there. She spoke to me in Italian.

'So it was you who took that poor cat to the vet? She is part of the colony I feed. I looked for her and wondered where she had gone.' She held out her hand. 'I am Antonella. Please come in, I would like to offer you coffee.'

Another cat lady! I followed her up a flight of stairs and into the *salotta*. The room was not large but was full of dark and heavy antique furniture. There was a big sideboard crowded with photographs, some of the family and many more of Jesus and Mary. A red velour cloth covered the long table, surrounded by a lot of chairs.

The room had a sense of an old-fashioned parlour, rarely used. Antonella brought small cups of black coffee and a plate of almond biscuits. I sensed a melancholy about her and her smile did not quite reach her eyes.

'I don't often sit in here, only when the family visits.'

As I wondered how seldom that might be, I made a pretence of sipping the coffee, wickedly black and strong. Yuck! Sicilians have a lethal relationship with caffeine. Not just a beverage, it is more like a constant companion. They find a way to enjoy a coffee on many occasions throughout the day. It might be meeting a friend for coffee, having a coffee for breakfast, one during a break at work, after lunch or after dinner. '*Vuole un caffe?*' – it is seen as rude not to accept the offer. There is a short story about a man who did the rounds of his Sicilian relatives and politely accepted their offer of coffee. He ended up drinking ten dark espressos and nearly had a caffeine-induced heart attack!

After a while we moved into the kitchen, hung with bunches of oregano picked from the country. It is fashionable in Britain to forage, though we used to just call it 'picking', but the Sicilians have been doing it for a long, long time. Nature offers a bounty free for the taking. In summer and autumn they pick thyme and mint, stock up on fennel seeds. From November to April, it's the season of foraging for wild greens: borage, bitter chicory, mustard tops, feathery fennel, wild asparagus and prickly nettles. Most of these greens are eaten simply steamed and dressed with olive oil. They're also used in salads and the pasta dish *bucatini* with wild greens and ricotta cheese.

Antonella wanted to show me how she prepared peppers, aubergines and pepperoncini in oil. Often served as part of an *antipasto*, they are not one of my favourites. But I sampled what she put on a plate and told her it was very good. I suspected that Antonella was one of those housewives who make their own pasta sauce using fresh local tomatoes. It would simmer for hours and probably be served at midday. Lunch is traditionally the most important meal in Sicily. Most shops close for the *pausa pranzo*, the lunch break between 13.00 and 16.00 hours. Typically, it consists of a first course (pasta, rice or similar), a second course (meat, fish or vegetables) and fruit.

Suddenly, all this talk of food took a different turn. Antonella's longing to confide was almost tangible.

'I have suffered a lot and sometimes I feel my only reason for being alive is the cats. They rely on me, you see. My husband was an alcoholic but he was told he shouldn't touch another drop.' She shrugged. 'I think when he goes out he does drink. And he smokes. How I hate the smell of smoke! I make him stand on the balcony.'

I gazed round the immaculate kitchen with everything in its place. But there was no soul about it and this woman seemed very lonely.

'We all used to live in this house,' she continued, 'the children, my mother. When Mamma died and I was out, my husband threw away all the photographs of her. He destroyed some of her furniture, too.'

I sat in silence and listened as all this came pouring out. It was as if she had never had anyone to tell before. Her eyes shone, as she stared around the kitchen. She seemed like a caged animal yearning to be free and to live. At last she was silent.

'Tell me about the cats,' I prompted.

'Ah, the cats!' she smiled. 'They are my babies. When I go out into the street with food they all come running. The grey cat is your cat's mother and the other black and white one, her sister. I have fed them since they were kittens. Poor beasts, so many people here dislike them and wish them harm. But what have they done? All they want is a bit of affection and enough food to eat.'

She paused and eyed me curiously. 'You paid the vet to treat that cat?'

I nodded.

'It must have cost a lot of money.'

I named the sum.

She shook her head. 'That was very good of you.'

'I can't bear to see anything suffering,' I replied. 'Someone had to help her.'

Antonella's gaze went to the crucifix hanging on the wall. 'I too cannot bear suffering,' she said.

A few days before I left for England I went back to Castelmola. I took the path that I now knew so well and there was Lizzie coming towards me. I opened a tin of Whiskas and she began to eat it. Then her mother, the pretty grey cat, arrived and tucked in. As I stroked Lizzie and took some photographs, I felt so happy. My little one could now lie and enjoy the sunshine. Her leg might never be the same again, but she was home with her mother and sister. I felt so glad I had restored her. Giulio had been right: she was returned to her world but there was a part of her that I liked to think remembered me, affectionate in her own way. All I could do now was pray she would be safe.

A woman approached with a rather strange-looking dog on a lead. The tips of its ears were missing and its coat was bald in places. She caught my gaze and shrugged. 'This dog could have been a *signor*,' she said, 'but he was badly treated when he was younger and so he is what he is.'

I told her about Lizzie and she said she believed that people who do not like animals like nothing in this world. She moved on. Then I caught sight of the young man who had helped me to find Giulio that afternoon.

He smiled broadly. 'I thought I heard you return that night to look for her, I saw the light of your torch. I am happy she is well.'

The sun shone down onto that little road and I stayed with Lizzie another half-hour. Those weeks in the apartment had somewhat tamed her and, now she was returned to her small domain, she allowed me to stroke her. I made to leave but came back again – I didn't want to go. In the end it was she who got up and strolled away down those steps, oblivious to the pain of my parting from her.

'Goodbye, Lizzie,' I said. 'Take care of yourself.'

There were tears in my eyes as I walked away.

TEN

We Love Them; But Do Cats Love Us?

A few months later I was back in Taormina. During the summer, I had sent several postcards to Antonella asking after Lizzie but had received no reply. I took it to mean that there was nothing to report. My little cat had resumed her feral existence.

Sicily had got into my blood again and, though I had a series of commissioned articles to work on throughout those months of 2002, I was restless. It was a fair English summer but I longed for the intensity of that Sicilian sun, the vivid blue sky. I contacted my landlady, Elke, and towards the end of September 2002, I returned to her apartment. It was as welcoming as ever, but as I walked up the slope towards Taormina centre, I began to wonder if it was a mistake to have come back so soon.

The sky was overcast, the atmosphere oppressive; not a leaf

stirred: Sirocco, the bane of Sicily's climate; that dry dust-laden wind, which blows from the Sahara. Although this was a dull day of cloud and mist, Sirocco can arise out of a clear sky and at any time of the year. It brings excessive humidity and an intolerable pressure of air that frays the nerves, sharpens the temper and, as many people claim, it affects their health. For some, and I am among them, it brings on a crushing sense of depression, making life seem hopeless, work meaningless, past and present a hideous mistake and the future ridiculous.

'There is no need to call a friend to make an appointment,' the Taorminese say, 'you just have to take a stroll along Corso Umberto and, at some point or other, you are bound to bump into them.'

Today that was precisely what I didn't want to do – I needed a little time alone to ease myself back into the exuberant Sicilian life. So I turned away and took the downward winding road that led to the Public Gardens. I wandered along the paths, identifying some of the flowers: there were French marigolds, amaryllis, those fountains of little red bellflowers that must have continued throughout the summer. There were still some roses and also Michaelmas daisies, a glorious cluster of them. Huge banana plants reared against the clear sky of a still-baking hot summer. They reminded me that this is a semi-tropical climate.

As I reached the end of the gardens I came across something I hadn't noticed before: it was Florence Trevelyan's dog cemetery. Two poignant inscriptions summed up the often incomprehensible, for Sicilians, British love of dogs.

Dear Fanny. Faithful Friend and Companion. Poisoned June 27 1899 aged 15 years.

Jumbo Perceval (Terrier) True Honourable Loving Little Friend and Helper.
September 3 1887 – Murdered July 24th 1904. Never Forgotten.

I turned back towards the entrance and saw an amazing sight: a cat had jumped up into the fountain and was sitting there, her tiny mouth wide open, catching the falling water. Tourists were gathered round and some took photographs. She continued drinking and drinking but when she had finished I think she felt a bit odd – perhaps she had taken in too much air.

'*Sera*,' a voice called and I turned to see that Maria had arrived.

She was weighed down with laden bags and I could see her legs were still troubling her. The cats had been waiting for her and milled around, their tails held upright, the ends slightly curved over. It is a signal of friendliness, I've learned. Kittens use this to greet their mother and adult cats continue to treat their favourite humans like a trustworthy mum, their tails held high. Cats who sense no hostility will greet each other with upright tails. A relaxed cat's tail curves down and back up in a gentle 'U'. The more interest she feels, the higher the tail. No doubt the interest here was Maria's supply of food.

It was clear that she loved cats in the way one loves little children.

'*Micio, micio,*' she murmured, as she filled their bowls.

But do cats love us? Or is this kind of show of affection cupboard love? True, they don't respond with the tail-thumping greeting of a dog when his owner returns. Research has shown canines experience positive emotions, like love and attachment, meaning that dogs have a level of sentience comparable to that of a human child. Cats are less demonstrative and some people dub them aloof. But surely it follows that, if a cat behaves in the same way towards certain human beings as she does towards other cats, then undoubtedly she is showing she is fond of her owner. Domesticated cats take this much further; they use kneading behaviour, the front paws treading on soft surfaces, a hark back to kittenhood. Kitten paws knead against the mother cat's breasts to induce milk to be released. Adult cats continue this behaviour when they're feeling most relaxed and content.

My cat, Sheba, has a habit of arriving on my pillow and kneading into my bare shoulder, purring loudly in my ear. When a cat throws herself on the ground at your feet and rolls around, she is asking for attention. Presenting her stomach in this way puts a cat in a vulnerable position so cats generally reserve the rolling around for people they trust and maybe love. The thing I love best about Sheba is her sometimes slow 'eye blink' from across the room; I have been honoured with a cat kiss.

The feral cats surrounding Maria while I mused on this were simply intent on having as much as they could of the pasta and fish mixture she was dispensing. They were silent. In contrast, domestic cats can be very talkative. Over time, Sheba has developed a number of meows to suit different occasions. They range from the little chirrup that greets me if I wake her when coming into a room to a plaintive high-pitched meow on her arrival in the house and not seeing anyone about. Then there is the quite desperate meow when she sees a packet of her food being opened. And of course there are the purrs. While these are sometimes a signal of comfort and contentment, research has shown that purring is an attempt to get something done. I remember my other cat Fluffy's loud and disconcerting purr, which I initially failed to recognise as a cry for help. New to the world of felines, I was unaware that they will purr when stressed or in distress or pain and are simply trying to attract attention.

The cats that Maria fed had no need of these niceties except perhaps for Lily, who had now settled herself on the elderly woman's lap while the others, having washed themselves, disappeared back into the garden.

I went to sit by her.

'How are things?' I asked.

She made the '*muh!*' shrug. 'Always the same, my neighbours are up to their usual tricks. As for these cats, they have done well enough during the summer. So many tourists feed them, but winter is coming. There will be rain and maybe those little ones won't survive.'

As I gazed at her large, work-worn hands passing over Lily's fur I sensed again the essential goodness in Maria and her love of these *trovatelle*, abandoned creatures; a devotion that marginalised her from the society she lived in.

'I am so sorry,' I said.

She gave me her lovely smile. '*Pazienza.*'

ELEVEN

I Glimpse the Dark Side of Sicily

Those small things restored me and I felt ready to face Taormina. In the evening I went in search of some Sicilian music, climbing the steps off the Corso that led to the Grotta di Ulisse. Someone grabbed my hand and I was whizzed right across the restaurant and unceremoniously plonked down at the table of an American couple who didn't seem to mind this intruder at all.

So we relaxed and talked. And my companions of this evening told me they had been all over Sicily to visit once again the Greek temples at Agrigento, the mosaics at Piazza Armerina. They had been to the island's 'navel' Enna, marvelling they had forgotten how splendid are those billowing hills of golden durum wheat, spent a day on the beach at Acireale, gazing at the rock, which in Greek mythology was hurled by the one-eyed giant into the sea.

'But the very best day,' commented Anna-Maria, 'was when we went back to "our" village. We drove into the country and watched my uncle's shepherd make the ricotta cheese and drank wine from his vineyard. For me, that is the real Sicily.'

'Does it make you want to come back here?' I asked.

'Maybe, one day, when we are old.'

In the meantime, there was America the wonderful, the bounteous to seduce them. They owned a hardware store, they told me, had loads of friends. The problem with coming back to Sicily, they added, was an ongoing family squabble over a piece of land.

'We need our space.'

Gaetano reached for his wallet and handed me his card. 'If ever you find yourself in Brooklyn, look us up.'

We joined in the general clapping to the music and I felt a wave of joy on hearing it again. The musicians might be playing for the tourists. They might, as one of the group told me, travel into Taormina from the surrounding villages because they needed to earn money to feed their families. One of them butted in to add that he had five children, think of how many mouths to feed. But there is something about the Sicilian when he plays and sings that is true to his nature. Reaping the corn, fishing by the light of sun or moon, riding a mule along the mountain path, his songs express emotions tinged with nostalgia and history. They come from the soul. There is '*La Terra Amara*' (The Bitter Earth), the earth that has sent him all over the world to escape the tyranny of earning his crust in agriculture; the resentful earth of Sicily demanding back-breaking work under a scorching sun, unyielding of water as a revenge for its deforestation. It is hard to believe that the rivers, especially the Simeto, Salso and Belice, were once navigable. Now they are silted up, or dry riverbeds, which are often used as rubbish dumps.

There came the mournful tremble of the mandolin, but not all these songs are melancholic. One of the best loved has the singer imitating the braying of a donkey. It might be corny, it might be calculated, but I'm an easy target. 'La Terra Amara', which nevertheless draws back so many Sicilians to their land, to this bitter earth.

The boom of the terracotta jar, the *quartara*, as the player twirled it in his hands and blew into it and the *fischietto*, a simple, three-stopped cane pipe, which in the right hands can produce a virtuoso of sound.

When I first heard this music, years ago, I found it all 'so romantic'. There were candles on the tables and painted jugs full of scarlet wine. Romantic! I could imagine that couple at the opposite table saying it in German, Dutch, Swedish: 'So romantic'. And that is what my wise Sicilian friends trade on. They have a commodity: *La Sicilia*! Blue seas and skies, wine and an excellent cuisine, why not sell it for the best price you can get?

Tonight it amused me to watch the German tourists pay an inflated price for local wine, clapping their hands and shouting 'Wunderbar!'

'Jenny?'

I glanced up and saw the owner, Filippo, had come to our table.

'There is something I have to tell you…'

His expression was grave. 'The cat, the one in Castelmola you took to the vet…'

His voice was almost drowned out by a loud burst of applause and I tried to concentrate.

'What is it?'

'She and many others were poisoned.'

I had a vision of the last time I had seen Lizzie, lying so contently, blinking in the sunlight. I brought my hands to my face. '*No!*'

'I'm sorry.'

Stricken, I was gazing at Filippo, trying to take in his words.

'Don't be sad,' he told me.

Don't be sad! When I felt the earth had shifted beneath me and I was falling into a black hole.

The music continued, people shouted and sang; they clapped their hands to its rhythms. I stayed on, there was nowhere else to go and I didn't want to be alone in the apartment. Then I remembered what Antonella had told me about the people in Castelmola who disliked cats. It must have been one of those who rolled poison into balls of meat and threw them down for the unsuspecting creatures to eat. I felt such a rage against them and the terrible act they had committed. Anger like this is fertile ground for notions of revenge but, as the night wore on and my fury turned to grief, I made up my mind I wouldn't leave it there.

Somehow I would help these cats.

TWELVE

Elke, Cat 'Mother' to a Myriad Felines

I had never realised that my landlady Elke was a *gattara* supreme until the day she invited me to visit her house. It was a few days after I'd received the devastating news of Lizzie, and I welcomed this diversion from my thoughts. She called me when, as usual, I was sitting with my coffee at the picture window.

'Come up and see my home.'

I knew that the property gazed out over the Ionian Sea, perched on the top of Capo Sant'Andrea, but I had never been able to discern exactly where or how you reached it.

'There's a little road that leads up on the left side of Isola Bella beach,' she told me. 'If you wait there, I'll come and fetch you.'

The tall gate swung open as if onto a magical domain where few people were admitted. Then came the slow drive along a rough road winding upward and flanked by rocky outcrops and the towering prickly pear. As we turned into the final stretch, Elke slowed the car to a crawl and I saw the reason why: several cats, which had been sunning themselves, scurried away. She led the way up a leafy-lined path into the garden: the lush beauty of a Mediterranean garden where pots spilled brilliant flowers and there was a straggle of ferns, roses, bougainvillea and that strange bird-like plant, the strelitzia. But most beautiful of all were the cats, so many of them: lurking in the shadows, skulking among plants, having a playful fight in a pool of sunlight. The garden was a cats' paradise. Tiny kittens regarded me with huge eyes, other cats pressed themselves against Elke's legs and she bent to talk to them, calling each by name. Found, saved or abandoned by uncaring people, these were the lucky cats who had found Elke. They had their own little shelters set among the plants and she fed them twice daily from her huge store of food kept in an old abandoned church in the grounds.

We moved into the house, awash with light as if it were an extension of Isola Bella, its terraces seeming to hang over the sea. Then I noticed all the same lovely touches that made my apartment so homely: the pretty cushions and throws over the rattan chairs, a fat tassel hanging from a basket. There were more cats, too: Freddi, fluffy pale-grey Nuovola and a huge ginger tom. They did not mix with the outdoor cats but carried on a luxurious existence in this cool interior.

This was a revelation for me. While I had been secretly caring for Lizzie, I had had no idea that Elke continually rescued all these felines.

Idyllic as this setting appeared, it was also one of violence and death. As we sat outside with a cold drink, Elke told me about the tomcats that grab hold of the females and bite holes in their necks to keep them still while they mate.

'So many of the kittens die. There are some nasty viruses in Sicily and their immune system isn't very strong. It's heartbreaking. You have to be strong if you do this kind of work.'

Later on I was to remember those words when I too encountered cruelty and fought death. And so I related a part of the story of Lizzie and how upset I was over the poisoning. I made no mention of the fact I had nursed her in the apartment.

Elke nodded. 'A lot of people here hate cats; they bring their children up to view them as a health risk. You should have brought her here.'

I felt terrible, guilty and terrible, but then how was I to know that Elke was also a *gattara*?

THIRTEEN

I Learn the Sad Fate of Lizzie

On the subject of the *gattare*, the sometimes mocked women who care for a number of cats, it certainly seems true there is a strong bond between the two. We go back a long way and have a lot in common, but perhaps the biggest thing we share is our history of being persecuted by the Church. After all we've been through, we have every reason to stick by each other.

In evolutionary terms the cat family is fairly modern, being only 3–5 million years old. They were domesticated, if you can ever say a cat is truly domesticated, by the Egyptians and considered, among other wild animals, to be the representatives on earth of gods and goddesses. One city in the Nile Delta had as its chief deity a woman with the head of a lioness called Bastet. She was attributed to sexual energy, fertility and child nurturing and her cult spread to other parts of Egypt. A wild and raunchy Bastet festival was held in April and May, attended by as many as 700,000 people and who knows how many cats. Ferals came to possess a special protected status in Egypt and it was a capital offence to kill one, even by accident.

But the fortunes of felines had changed radically by the late Middle Ages. From being lauded as symbols of motherhood, they were dubbed agents of the Devil and the companions of witches. Feline phobia reigned. This was largely because the established Church wanted to stamp out all traces of pagan religions and cults. From the twelfth to the fourteenth centuries, both women and cats were persecuted for their so-called involvement in witchcraft. A solitary female who believed in natural remedies and had as her sole companion an amiable puss cat would be denounced by suspicious neighbours and hauled before a court. There are stories of animals being put on trial, too.

Along with this hatred of cats came an element of hatred of women, in particular the link between female sexuality and the sexual habits of female cats. The very quality of fertility admired by the ancient Egyptians was to be condemned and stamped out by the early Christian Church.

In these so-called enlightened times it is awful to imagine a single and perhaps lonely woman with her cat companion judged and horribly put to death. But then perhaps things have not changed to such a large degree when I think of Maria, whose neighbours spited her in every way they could and gossiped about her strangeness just because of her love of cats.

I longed to talk to someone about the death of Lizzie

and the rest of her colony. There were so many questions I needed to ask. The person who could best answer them was Antonella and yet I kept putting off that bus journey to Castelmola. A few days before I was due to return to England, I couldn't procrastinate any longer. When the bus drew into the park, I hesitated again, feeling anxious, afraid of what I was going to hear. In Castelmola, I set off down the streets and for a moment lost my way until I saw the now familiar slope downwards to Via Canone. It was strangely deserted with not a sign of a cat but for Lizzie's mother and another small feline. Several times I rang on Antonella's bell but there was no reply. I was beginning to think I would have to leave a note when I heard footsteps and saw her approaching. She was delighted to see me.

'How did it happen?' I asked the question I'd asked myself so many times.

'I received your postcards,' Antonella said. 'When the first arrived she was always on the street and doing well with a hint of a limp. I had planned to send you a photograph but then she disappeared.'

'When did it happen?'

'It must have been in July.'

July! All those weeks I had felt happy that Lizzie was living a good life when, in fact, she was dead.

'The first cat was found lying in the street near that old house and afterwards in various parts of Castelmola. They had a curious appearance as if they were made of stone. When I heard what had happened, I ran around looking for your cat but I couldn't find her. I have never been able to find her.'

So the mystery remained of what happened to Lizzie. Had she escaped the poisoning? Or had she run off to hide and die a miserable death?

'I kept on expecting her to turn up,' Antonella continued, 'but she never has.'

She took me to a piece of wasteland, where two of the cats she fed were playing. 'It is so easy to wrap the poison in a bit of meat and throw it down here, no one would know who it was who had done it. The world is a horrible place and sensitive people like us have to suffer so much – we have to take on the sins of the world.'

I remembered the crucifix in her house. 'It is hard to be sensitive,' I noted.

Then Antonella confided: 'I have some idea who has done this but I cannot report them because I don't have proof. However, there was this woman who complained about the mess the cats made round her house and then two days later they were dead.'

I could see she didn't want me to leave, enjoying the company of another human being who felt as she did. We kissed and hugged, and I said I would come again. As the bus drew away, I stared out of the window, shocked and upset. I had believed Lizzie was in good hands but, as Antonella said, no one would have guessed that is what these people could do.

It was a sad journey down to Taormina.

FOURTEEN

Giovanni, the Man Who Loves Flowers

*T*he first Saturday morning of October, early: the Public Gardens. It is all so lovely and fresh; I feel full of hope, in the moment. I have an appointment to meet the botanist Giovanni Bonier. He arrives with his bulldog, Bimbo, who is very interested in the cats. They arch their backs and spit at him, run up trees and glare – in particular, a large black one. In contrast, Bimbo seems an amiable bulldog who only wants to play.

It is the perfect morning to be strolling along these well-remembered paths striped with the now lengthening shadows. The sun has begun to relax its grip on the earth, the light is softer; there is a subtle change of colour on the mountains and on the sea. I love every season in Sicily, but perhaps autumn best.

I am to have a guided tour of the flowers. As Giovanni

explains, they come from all over the world, the names as sumptuous as the plants themselves.

There is *Capparis spinosa*, part of the caper family, whose small buds are picked as a relish. Then Cuphea from the Greek '*kyphos*', which means 'curved', alluding to the curved fruit capsule; it has sprays of orange-red tubular flowers.

Every plant has its history. Here is the Bird of Paradise, the strelitzia, named after Charlotte of Mecklenburg-Strelitz, wife of George III. Its name is apt, the three-sepalled, two-petalled blooms curiously resembling an exotic bird's head. There is the Jacaranda, its name originating from the Brazilian/Indians. This variety, *Mimosifolia*, has numerous leaflets and small purple blue flowers with a white throat.

The nuts of the mandorla (or almond) tree are used widely in Sicily for all kinds of confectionery. This variety is the *Prunus dulcis* (Asia minor), easy to spot with its very dark bark and pink flowers.

Brugmansia sanguinea lives up to its name, with its bright-red 'Angel's Trumpets'. Originally, these flowers were used by the American Indians as a hallucinogen; it takes its title from another 'name' in natural history: Justine Brugmans, who lived from 1763 to 1819.

Salvia leucantha is a white version of the more familiar fiery red Sage. The stamens of its flowers work on a rocket mechanism: the visiting bee has pollen pressed onto its head as it pushes against a sterile projection from the anther. The word 'salvia' means to heal or save. Used herbally, it is medically approved in Germany. Extracts taken internally have been recommended for anxiety, insomnia and digestive problems. It is sometimes used externally for insect bites and infections of the throat, mouth and skin.

London apothecary John Parkinson (1567–1650) gave his name to *Parkinsonia*. The more popular name is the Jerusalem Thorn – a spiny shrub with little sprays of yellow, pea-like flowers, dotted with orange. It comes from Central America.

We pause by a huge cedar tree, magnificent with its blue-green, needle-like leaves, but, as Giovanni explains, it is overshadowing other plants and drawing all the strength from the soil. Lofty though it is, he feels it ought to come down.

I ask him what it is like to be young and educated and living in Sicily. As a botanist he gives me an analogy in plant life: the roots of a kind of fatalistic thinking are planted so deep that it is impossible, in his opinion, to change it: 'They cannot see the big picture, cannot get together. Each has his own point of view and won't compromise.'

The garden is a mishmash of different periods. There are trees that Florence Trevelyan almost certainly brought from the East and many rare plants and flowers, which should stay exactly where they are. But there are others planted without any forethought and these should be severely pruned or taken out. He points out plants in the wrong places, such as the sun-loving hibiscus positioned among those plants that enjoy the shade.

The pavilions, designed by Florence Trevelyan, were christened 'the beehives'. They were made of a variety of materials, from stonework facing in varying cuts and dimensions at the base to alternating brickwork and the lava-stone detail of the turrets to rustic logs on the little balconies and jetties. Now they are being allowed to fall into ruins. There is also the 'Alice in Wonderland' behaviour of those who tend the parterre, which is a mixture of stones and bricks. Giovanni explains wryly that the gardeners spend hours sweeping it with old-fashioned bristle brooms. A machine exists, but it is not used.

We come to the cactus garden, where I say that I think it's not in keeping with the rest of the garden. Giovanni agrees with me.

'It has always taken outsiders to get things done here,' he explains. 'We've been colonised by so many different invaders, but, although the people have been enriched by their civilisations, they have never gone on to develop these ideas. [Di Lampedusa's classic] *The Leopard* says it all. In spite of that, I wouldn't live anywhere else. The climate is perfect. And I am not an employee of the council but a consultant so not as answerable, even if sometimes one feels unappreciated. When I first started to work in the gardens I catalogued all the flowers. But do you see any labels?'

'There are two kinds of people,' he adds. 'You give some money, they eat the lot; you give it to others, of course they eat some of it but they do something with the rest.'

And so we continue, I to smile with delight, he to list all these flowers: the datura white, yellow cream and rose striped, purple Salvia, bright-yellow tagetes, the roses and hibiscus. Giovanni is a mine of information. There is the fascinating Dragon tree with its small, fragrant flowers. The resin from its stems is the source of 'dragon's blood' used in varnishes and photo engraving. Good that it is here – in the wild this elegant tree is endangered due to overexploitation.

We gaze up into the odd whorled branches of the Araucaria

(the Monkey Puzzle tree); its leaves are whorled too. The fruiting cones take several years to develop and, as they mature, they break up. And here is a ginger tree, Zingiber, sounding straight from Edward Lear. The rhizomes of this species are used for the many kinds of ginger we find in the shops: fresh, green or root, crystallised, dried. Another variety, Alpinia, has three large, lobal lower lips.

But what is the name of 'my' beautiful weeping shrub, which I've stopped to admire since May? Russelia, Giovanni tells me, named after Dr Alexander Russell – sometimes 'coral plant', 'fire cracker' or 'fountain plant'. It has pendant stems, simple leaves and two-lipped, five-lobal flowers that go on and on.

We part by the new statue given to the town hall by sculptor Piero Guidi in the previous year: two travellers cast in antique bronze sit on the bench by the entrance gates. Her head leans on his shoulder; she has a small case.

The only strange thing about them is that both sprout a full set of wings.

FIFTEEN

I Launch Catsnip

I could not get Lizzie out of my mind. That image of her lying in the sunshine with contented, half-closed eyes kept returning. Back in England, well-meaning friends tried to tell me to put it behind me: they had similar stories to recount of holidays in Mediterranean countries where they too had come across hungry or sickly cats.

'You do what you can while you're there but, when you leave, you have to put it out of your mind. You'd drive yourself crazy, otherwise.'

But I couldn't forget. The anger I'd felt that night at the Grotta di Ulisse renewed whenever I thought of the dreadful deed some animal hater had committed. If I could do something to help these feral cats, then Lizzie's death would not have been in vain.

So what should I do? What was really at the core of this

cruelty towards animals, which appeared to extend through-out the Mediterranean countries? It wasn't the first time I had come across it. Travelling in Cyprus, Greece and Tunisia always there were skinny and sickly cats that appeared by magic the moment you sat down at a restaurant table; always unfeeling waiters, who chased them away.

'Next time we'll take a holiday where there aren't any cats!' Andrew would sigh.

But there were always cats and the visits to a local super-market to buy tins of tuna, always the awareness that sooner or later, I had to leave them to their fate. Lizzie, I realised, represented a symbol, awakening my energy to act. But I didn't know how to begin. And then something quite fortuitous happened.

Not long after my return from Sicily, I'd met up with a photographer friend, also called Jenny, to discuss feature ideas for our county magazine, *Sussex Life*.

'There's always something happening in Brighton,' I said. 'Why don't we offer a series of monthly features on the 24/7 City?'

My friend was enthusiastic.

'If they commission us,' I added, 'it would mean that some months we'd be up at an unearthly hour.'

'It will be fun,' she smiled.

I sometimes reminded her of that remark when we talked to the homeless at midnight, or shivered in Brighton Market at four in the morning. But it was the 10pm slot that was the catalyst for me.

A white Vauxhall Combo came to a halt outside Hove station. On its side was the distinctive logo of the Cats

Protection League. Beverley Avey, Welfare Officer for the Brighton and Hove City branch, waved us aboard and off we went. A stray, unneutered black cat and her three kittens had been sighted in a Hove garden. Our mission tonight was to catch them.

'We have so many calls from people telling us of cats seen in the neighbourhood scavenging for food,' Beverley explained as we drove through the night. 'Owners move away and just leave their pets behind, believing they will fend for themselves. Cats are not as stand-offish and self-sufficient as people think, they crave love and attention.'

She told us she was never really off-duty. Working late into the night, she juggled this with being a wife and mother, as well as holding down a job.

'I come home to find the answer machine jam-packed with messages. Calls range from lost cats to reports of ill treatment or accidents, to those who have given one of "our" cats a home and want to report on its progress. Other people have decided they don't want their cat anymore and can we take it on.'

Felines are twilight creatures so our best chance of catching them was now. We knocked on the door and the owner led us through to the garden. I carried the food, strong-smelling pilchards, and Beverley lugged in the trap. Unlike the one I had seen Giulio use, this was sprung by remote control. It meant we could sit a distance away, ready to press the switch when or if the cats took the bait. So we sat on a garden bench in the darkened garden and prepared for a long wait.

Beverley stifled a laugh. The house owner had apparently let her own cat out and, notoriously curious as felines are, this one was sniffing around the trap. We managed to pick him up and take him indoors.

While we waited, Beverley told us about some of her latest cases. There was Luca, who waited patiently outside his so-called family's house to be let in until he collapsed. When he came to Beverley, he wouldn't eat for some time. Happily, he decided there was life beyond his first unkind owners and was now being fostered.

The week before, Beverley had collected two very small kittens, which had been shut inside a shed for a week.

'They were desperately hungry and crying so pitifully until I squirted syringes of kitten milk into their mouths. It was a miracle they had survived that long.'

When a lovely surrogate mother called Trina accepted them as her own, this resulted in a story with a happy ending.

'There won't be much difficulty finding pretty little kittens like those a home,' she went on. 'Older cats have so much to offer, although they are never as popular. They have a wonderful serenity about them and are truly the ultimate stress busters, if only people would give them a chance.'

Suddenly, we were on the alert: a shadow darker than the gloom of the night was making its way towards the trap. And another... Beverley pressed the switch and the door clanged closed.

They didn't like it, not one bit. Their big green eyes gazed at us through the bars and I tried to tell them we were doing this for all the right reasons. But they weren't listening; instead, they were leaping about, trying to escape.

We decided to call it a night. As Beverley said, Mum and

her other kitten had been alerted and would now give the trap a wide berth. She would return the following evening.

We drove towards Brighton, where fosterer Jo was waiting. Beverley had a team of people who were prepared to take on cats and kittens and care for them on a short-term basis. Jo led the way outside to her tiny garden, which she had given over to a series of purpose-built pens. Released, the kittens shot out of the trap, understandably freaked by this transition. One of them climbed up to the roof and then hung there, wondering how to get down. As Jo said, in a couple of days they would have calmed down and realised they were in receipt of lots of TLC.

Over a cup of tea, Beverley outlined the huge problem Brighton and Hove has with cats.

'So many people won't have them neutered and so they continue to breed. Did you know that one cat can be responsible for 20,000 descendants in five years?'

No, I didn't, but I was learning fast.

Beverley shares her home with eight cats, not to mention several felines in the pen near the back door. Further down the garden is a log cabin, which her long-suffering husband imagined would be an office. Here, there are more cats, like the aptly named Angel.

'I can't turn them away,' she explains, fondling Boris, a cat that wasn't rescued but decided to move across the road from his former home. 'And the joy they give in return makes it all worthwhile.

'But I still find it hard to talk about William, a lovely old gentleman. He needed permanent medication for a kidney problem and I had terrible misgivings about letting him go.

'I was persuaded by someone who vowed he loved cats and would give William a good home. When this man's girl-friend returned to him, he moved out of his house and left the helpless cat to its fate. William crept into a cardboard box and died. I shall never forgive nor forget.'

There was such a passion in her voice. An echo of how I had felt, that evening sitting in the Grotta di Ulisse, when Filippo had brought me the news of Lizzie's death. It was late but I couldn't leave without telling her my story.

'I can't get her out of my mind,' I finished. 'I'm so angry about the way these people treat cats and I just feel I've got to do something about it.'

Beverley listened and nodded. 'I know exactly how you feel.'

'But Sicily,' my friend Jenny put in, 'surely that's a bit crazy?'

'Do it,' Beverley said decisively. 'Someone has to help them.'

It was nearly midnight before Jenny and I started on the drive home but I had made up my mind.

Beverley's words rang in my ears: 'If only cats were neutered the numbers would reduce and they would be chosen by those who really want to offer a loving home.'

'It all stems from overpopulation,' animal welfare campaigner Suzy Gale confirmed. 'None of these countries has an efficient neutering programme for feral animals; consequently, they breed at an overwhelming rate. The mother cats are weakened by continuously giving birth and the kittens too are sickly. And local people seem to think the only method of control is to kill them.'

I'd come across Suzy as I researched people who worked for cats. For several years she had organised and carried out a neutering programme in Cyprus and had achieved a great deal in controlling the colonies.

'It involves a lot of hard work and heartbreak, too,' she told me. 'But if you decide to have a go, I'm happy to advise you.'

Brighton isn't called breezy for nothing. As you step out of the railway station and start down Queens Road, you receive a blustery greeting. That autumn of 2002, it was particularly wild, with high winds and rough seas; the poor old West Pier took another battering. By the end of the year, part of it collapsed, the beginning of the end. One man was swept out to sea, having clung to the girders underneath the pier and called for help. I battled my way to a cosy tearoom, where I met another cat lady, Angela Collins. The world was beginning to appear thronging with these feisty women who took it on themselves to do something practical for felines.

Angela's project, Care 4 Cats, concentrates on the Balearic Islands, where she has made considerable inroads into controlling the cat population.

'Several years ago, I was on holiday in Ibiza,' she told me. 'I was horrified to discover the many thousands of stray cats and kittens all over the island, having either been abandoned, or born on the street. There was no help for them, and they were simply left to die of starvation or diseases such as cat flu, leukaemia, AIDS and enteritis.'

This sad situation preyed on Angela's mind and so she decided to try to do something about alleviating it. In the Millennium year she set up Care 4 Cats and the charity began its work of neutering these strays to decrease the population in a humane way. She echoed Suzy Gale's words.

'It's an uphill battle and you have to be prepared for local opposition. Sometimes you get so downhearted when they just don't seem to understand what you are trying to do.'

I was to remember this advice during my own struggles in the years ahead, but at that time and with the poignant image of Lizzie in mind, I refused to see obstacles; I was determined to go ahead. If they could do it, so could I.

So what should I call my project? It's been shown that people prefer words that are easy to pronounce and understand. My search revealed that many such names had already been taken. Finally, I plumped for Catsnip, liking the play on the words 'cat snip'. I opened a building society account and set about raising funds. I'd never done anything like that before and I soon discovered it wasn't easy. Take car boot sales, for example. I began by taking a stall at my local community centre. This proved to be a steep learning curve. I arrived early for my first sale, with a pretty cloth to lay over my table and set about arranging my goods. I'd scarcely finished when a fat woman arrived.

'New to this, are you?' she demanded, picking up and examining some pieces of porcelain donated by a friend.

'I thought the doors didn't open till ten,' I said.

'Oh, I'm not the public! My stall is over there.'

She held up a pretty glass, one of a set of six. 'I'll give you a couple of quid for these,' she smiled, showing a missing tooth. 'Take them off your hands.'

I hadn't priced the glasses but instinct told me they were worth more than that.

'I'm selling them for a pound each,' I said, surprised at how firm I could be.

The smile faded. 'Well, I hope you get it,' retorted the woman and waddled away.

I'd learned my first lesson. Seasoned car boot sellers will often prowl the other stalls, trying to pick up a bargain, which they can sell on for a lot more at their own pitch.

On another occasion someone had donated a collection of costume jewellery – necklaces, bracelets and earrings. I'd brought in a mirror, which I propped against the wall so that people could try them on. There was one woman whom I swear tried on every piece and took her time about it. I struggled to keep my eye on her while I served other customers, but not long after she had gone I found a pair of earrings was missing too. Lesson number two: car boot sales can be very susceptible to thieves. Far better if you can persuade a friend to help out, otherwise you're also stuck behind your table without the chance of a break.

I'd embarked on these sales with the idealism of a missionary but I soon discovered that, never mind my worthy cause, these canny shoppers were set on knocking the prices down to as low as they could get. They weren't prepared to pay more than thirty pence for a paperback and were quick to point out if they thought one looked a bit dog-eared, lowering their offer to twenty-five pence. Sometimes they were simply out to swindle. It still hurts to remember Weasel, the name I gave to the tall, thin man who arrived at my stall shortly after the public had been let in.

'Got any books?' His tone was nasal.

As a matter of fact, I had a large number of them. Some

friends I'd known from our days of demonstrating against live animal exports had cleared out their attics. There was a large box of them I had yet to sort through.

Weasel laughed, an unpleasant sound. 'Oh, don't worry about that! Let me have a quick look at them.'

At that moment, a young woman arrived who had read my poster and wanted to know more about Catsnip. Her eyes filled with tears when I told her about the death of Lizzie.

'I don't want to buy anything,' she said, 'but here's something for your funds.'

I was still basking in the fact someone had shown an interest when I realised Weasel was holding out a five-pound note.

'I've had a quick look,' he said. 'And I'd like to buy this little lot.' He opened a large checked bag, where I could see about five books already stowed inside. 'I think that should cover them.'

And he was off, his long, thin body slithering into the crowd, and I was left with a strong feeling I'd been cheated. There was something about his manner, the swift, practised way he had gone through those books and packed them away that convinced me they were far more valuable than the price he'd paid for them. After that I was always careful to examine every donation before I put it on sale.

Those car boot sales were mortifying, threatening to crush my enthusiasm for my project. The final straw came when, after spending hours on hand-stitching a series of cushion covers, absolutely no one showed the slightest interest. I calculated my overall takings, £67.13p. That wouldn't take me far. So I turned my back on the community centre and decided to try something else.

Time was passing and, if I wanted to launch Catsnip the following year, I'd have to get a move on. Perhaps selling wasn't for me. I was, after all, a journalist and writing was my forte. Suzy's voice came into my mind.

'We contacted various charities and some of them were very good in giving us a grant. I can give you a list, if you like.'

The letter writing came easily enough and I was able to explain my aims clearly: 'to take a team of vet, nurse and helpers to Sicily to treat and neuter feral cats, considering that the local authorities do nothing to ameliorate the problem'. I also had to fill in application forms, something I more than dislike but seem to have a block about. Nevertheless, I put my head down and soon they were in the post.

I wrote articles about Lizzie's story and one of them appeared in a little magazine called *Animals' Voice*. Betty, Jayne and Tracy are three wonderful women who rescue and care for wildlife in the New Forest area of Hampshire. Their magazine covers all kinds of animal issues and they were kind enough to include mine. The response was excellent; I was so touched by the readers' letters. Often women, they were by no means wealthy but sent me what they could afford. The balance in my building society grew and, when I received substantial cheques from three of the charitable organisations I had written to, I knew I could go ahead.

So I phoned Elke, my landlady. Before I had left Taormina we had had a long talk and she had agreed to help in any way she could.

'How's the weather?'

'Don't mention it,' I replied. 'We are having awful wind and rain.'

'It's sunny here,' came the cheery voice, 'not all that warm, but sunny.' She laughed. 'But you don't want to talk about the weather! How are you doing?'

'Good news, I'm ready to start planning the trip,' I told her. 'I have the money but I don't know where we can operate. I've asked my vet if he'd be part of the team, but he's busy.'

There was silence for a moment. Elke was obviously absorbing this.

'I have an idea,' she said at last. 'Remember Ines, the woman who lived in the downstairs apartment where you stayed?'

Yes, I remembered her, a rather eccentric German woman but undoubtedly a lover of cats. I'd heard her calling them in to be fed, every evening.

'She has a summerhouse – it's big and secluded. It would be the perfect place. No one would see what we were doing.'

'And the vet?'

'Leave it with me, I'll see what I can do.'

Within days she was back to me. Yes, Ines had said we could use the summerhouse and she had managed to persuade an American friend who was a vet to volunteer his services. All I had to do was pay for his flight from the States. Frank Caporale was on board.

That year, I hardly noticed Christmas. The moment it was over I began to assemble the equipment I would need. There were traps and cages to order, which would be sent by road and delivered upon my arrival in Sicily. Guy, my sister's vet, had given me a list of the drugs and other things I would need for the 'surgery'. As the idea of this project took shape, I became increasingly bolder in asking people to give me things. I wrote to several drug companies and some of them donated necessary medicines. My local hospital in Worthing offered forceps and scissors. Other equipment I had to buy from veterinary supply firms.

Daffodils appeared in my garden and the days lengthened. There were copies of the May 2003 Brighton Festival brochure in the library. Sometimes I despaired I would ever be ready in time. During the week before I left England, I was still rushing round collecting last-minute supplies. Finally, I was faced with the problem of how to get the drugs and surgical supplies from the UK to Sicily. And here I must say my ignorance proved a blessing: I had absolutely no idea of the nature of ketamine, the drug used by vets in the absence of inhalant anaesthetic. I knew nothing about its use as a recreational drug, stronger than the same amount of speed or coke and with unpredictable effects. Drug taking has never appealed to me, though I do enjoy a glass of good wine. Where I was concerned, it was just one item on my list of veterinary drugs and I treated it as such. Of course, I know better now and I shudder to think of what I was doing when I packed everything into a large box, covered it with brown paper and labelled it 'SICILIAN CAT WELFARE'.

SIXTEEN

Operation Catsnip

*O*n the morning of my departure I unloaded the box from the taxi boot and onto a trolley to trundle it through to check in. The man at the desk took one glance at it and said it would have to travel as an oversized parcel. He didn't ask what was inside. I don't want to imagine the almost certainly different scenario in these days of high security. As I watched it disappear into the chute I heaved a sigh of relief, but again I was unaware of any risk I had run. On the plane I relaxed and ordered a glass of wine – I was on my way.

Eleven years ago, Catania airport was quite small and I don't remember much in the way of security. When my oversized parcel appeared on the carousel, I snatched it off and handed it over to the waiting taxi driver. Off we went, through Catania, with its Baroque buildings, wide avenues and squares, splendid churches and monasteries. The city was repeatedly destroyed over the centuries by eruptions of Etna. In 1693, a massive earthquake levelled much of it, but its citizens bounced back, using lava stone to create an even better city. An aura of the eighteenth century still lingers over much of its heart.

Every year, for three days, the streets of Catania surge with thousands of people following the procession of their beloved patron saint, Agatha. The second evening, 4 February, is probably the most emotional when, after a sleepless night, thousands of Catanese crowd the cathedral at dawn to greet the image of their saint as she is carried to the high altar and then placed, by the faithful, in a silver carriage. The figure borne high above the crowd is adorned with jewels donated by celebrities and sovereigns, including a cross that was given by the composer Vincenzo Bellini. This spectacle, which combines cult devotion and tradition, is almost unique in the world.

For centuries the people of Catania have looked upon Saint Agatha as their protector in times of trouble. On AD 1 February 252, a year after the young Christian woman was martyred, the story goes that a violent eruption was miraculously halted by holding up the virgin's veil. Since then, the people of Catania have turned to the veil to conquer the menace of Etna. In 1444, and again during the catastrophic eruption of the seventeenth century, it appeared to stop the threatening flow of lava. Indeed, the veil continues to be brandished against the volcano to the present day.

We turned our backs on Catania, then took the familiar snaking roads that lead upwards to Taormina and, at last, turned into the little road leading to Elke's house. She was waiting at the gate, looking glamorous as ever with her mass of blonde curly hair and wonderful smile.

'I've made it!' I laughed and we fell into each other's arms.

The huge parcel was unloaded and carried into the house.

'I can't believe you got that thing through!' Elke marvelled. 'There must have been an angel watching over you.'

In retrospect, I think that might well have been true.

As I stood on her terrace, gazing out over the sea glittering in the afternoon sunshine, I could hardly believe I had done it. All those months of planning had been a success. There I was in Taormina, poised to begin my adventure.

Once more I sat in Elke's comfortable room with her cats. Nellie, Freddi, Nuovola and Giulio strolled about, sniffing at this visitor. I stayed with Elke overnight and we chatted over a leisurely breakfast; I was getting to know her better and liking what I found. I told her about my childhood in Surrey, the house with the big garden and all our animals.

'My mother really preferred dogs, I think, but my father was crazy about cats. We had one called Ginger; he was my special cat and I cried for days when someone poisoned him. We suspected neighbours who had a mentally retarded son but we had no proof. There was another, a tortoiseshell who was constantly having kittens, but I suppose people didn't think so much about neutering then as they do now.'

Elke refilled our coffee cups.

'I was five months old when my father, a medical doctor, was called up by the Army to work during the Second World War,' Elke told me. 'I grew up in the little German town of Westphalia, and as we were so close to the industrial part of Germany, heavy bombing started after a few years. My parents had a little rough-haired dachshund and that was my first love for an animal. Every night our town was bombed and we all had to sleep in bunk beds in the basement. I had an upper bunk and took the little trembling dog into my bed. I would tell Biene, that was her name, in English Bee: "Let us fall fast asleep so we don't hear the airplanes coming, the whistle of the bombs falling down, and we will not realise if we should get hit." Thank God we did not.

'In 1945, my mother took my three sisters and me to friends in Bavaria. She thought that it would be safer there than in Westphalia. We lived on a farm with cows, pigs, chicken and sheep. I loved the calves and I found out how good fresh cow milk tastes. But I also saw how cruelly they killed chickens and poor piggies. I felt so sorry for them, but I guessed it had to be like that.

'I made friends with a little mouse and brought some food to it. One day I took it in my hand, but the mouse did not like that and bit me on my little finger. That's how I learned that we also have to be cautious with animals.

'When I was about twelve or thirteen we moved into a nearby town. My father had come back late from war and prison. Every day on my way back from school, I met this beautiful shepherd dog; she was thin and very hungry and seemed not to belong to anybody. I always fed her some bread and we would sit together and I had to caress her. I found out that she belonged to a sick man in the neighbourhood and, when he died, she disappeared. Somebody must have taken her away. I was very, very sad not to see my good friend anymore.'

Two women sitting in a garden, sharing their childhood affection for animals: one German, one English, whose countries were once at war. The love of animals transcends nationality and all the other categories we rely on to define ourselves. And the human–animal bond touches the deepest parts of our heart and emotions.

'So, what brought you to Sicily in the first place?' I was curious to know.

'After I finished school I studied at an aviation school in Frankfurt in 1956. In those years it was very prestigious to become an air steward or reservations clerk. At the end of my studies I was taken on by Lufthansa, which was just coming into service again after the war, to work in the main office in Frankfurt. Here, I met my future husband, the Marchese Emilio Bosurgi from Messina, Sicily. His family owned the most important citrus essence distillery in Europe at that time.

'When Pan American started to fly Boeing 707 from New York to Europe, I was employed as an air stewardess – such a good job in those times. Then I met my future mother-in-law and she offered me a good job in her industry as her public relations person. Not many people spoke languages at that time in Sicily and her company had international customers. The most important one was Coca-Cola USA, customers for lemon oil, which they needed for their basic syrup, sent all over the world. In those days I lived in a beautiful palazzo in Messina…'

Intrigued, I wanted to know what happened next, but at that moment Elke glanced at her watch.

'Oh, look at the time! I have to be in Taormina by ten. If you can get your things together, I'll drop you off at the apartment.'

I should have to wait patiently for the next instalment of Elke's story.

'Take tomorrow to settle in,' she advised, as we bumped our way down the stony path. 'Then, when the traps and cages arrive, we can start getting the summerhouse ready.'

She dropped me off in little Via Guardiola Vecchia and I let myself in. Once again I sat at the picture window, gazing down onto Isola Bella and marvelling yet again at the view. The sun danced over the sea in a myriad points of light, the blue flowers of the plumbago hung over the sunlit path. It felt like coming home.

Next day, I wondered anxiously whether the traps and cages would arrive. What would I do if there was a hitch? Time passed and I was on tenterhooks. It was halfway through the afternoon before I heard the sound of a large van drawing up in the street below and I rushed down to direct the driver up to the terrace.

Then it was down to work. Elke's friend Ines opened up the summerhouse and we covered a large table with plastic sheeting and laid out the drugs, instruments and dressings. Another table was organised for the operations. The summerhouse boasted its own bathroom, which made us self-contained. Elke brought in high-powered lights, bowls for the sterilising liquid and the ever-welcome kettle. What a transformation! We stood gazing round with something like disbelief.

'All set,' said Elke.

On 6 June, Frank Caporale, the vet, together with Ross, a doctor who was to assist him, flew in from the USA. Elke had organised dinner at a small seaside restaurant and we were all in high spirits as we tucked into pizza washed down with red wine.

'I hear you're into drug smuggling, Jenny,' Frank teased. 'It must have been those innocent blue eyes that fooled them.'

'Oh, there's more to Jenny than you know!' Elke joined in the joke.

I shook my head. 'I honestly didn't know about ketamine,' I protested.

Which made them laugh even louder.

Frank leaned over and refilled my glass. 'Come on, folks, she's done a great job!' He raised his glass and the others followed.

'To Jenny!'

This was my first experience of Frank's gentle kindness. I glimpsed it many times during that week as we worked in the summerhouse for he treated every cat as an individual and kept a careful watch on them after their operations; they might have been his own pets. He was always calm and reassuring when I was upset by the effect of ketamine injections. Many of the cats seemed to go on a 'trip', jerking around the cage until they finally fell asleep.

'It looks worse than it is,' he told me. 'They won't remember anything when they wake up.'

I knew I had to believe him.

'And think how much better lives they'll have without constantly having kittens.'

Now I agreed wholeheartedly with that.

Our main problem was to sustain the supply of cats. Frank was highly skilled and worked very quickly. He told us he was prepared to operate day and night, if we could bring in the cats.

Every morning Elke and I went off with the traps in search of colonies. Earlier, she had visited the various cat ladies in the beach areas and explained what we were going to do. They were ready and very willing to help but the cats were not so cooperative. Catching a feral cat is a waiting game. They were very wary of the traps, even though there were tasty morsels waiting inside, but gradually their curiosity got the better of them and we would hear the satisfying snap as the door came down behind them. Then, with a towel thrown over the top to quieten them, we rushed back to the summerhouse to unload them into carriers before returning to start all over again. In this way we covered a large area, clambering up and down the steps that led to the beach, crouched behind a convenient wall to wait for our next customers.

Angela was one of our most dedicated helpers. Her love for cats verged on the fanatical and she threw herself unsparingly into this work. She was a small skinny woman, who battled constantly with her mother over this devotion. *Mamma* resented her taking any time away from the restaurant they ran together.

'Don't let her know I'm going out with you again this morning,' Angela pleaded, 'or she'll fly into a terrible temper.'

We were treated to an example of this, one day, when the older woman stood on the terrace of the restaurant, screaming at her daughter, careless of her startled customers, who did not understand Sicilian and hadn't a clue what was going on.

'Angela's wearing herself out,' Elke remarked. 'She eats like a sparrow and pushes herself to the extreme.'

Certainly, she looked exhausted, with dark circles under

her eyes. She had a permanently anxious expression and agonised over every cat she caught. When one of her own cats died, she was inconsolable.

'I should have done more, I should have done more,' she wailed.

'Have you had something to eat?' Elke, always concerned for other people, asked.

Angela nodded. 'I've had an apple.'

'You need to keep yourself strong,' I added. I myself had suffered from anorexia in the past and could read the signs.

Diligent as she was, Angela taught me a valuable lesson: anyone who works for animals needs to safeguard their own health or they become weak and good for nothing, thus defeating the object. We have to accept our limitations – no one person can solve the problem, find loving homes for every animal, or rescue every wild creature in distress. Yet together we can make a huge difference and change the world for the better, one animal at a time.

The story of the starfish effect sums it up. A man is walking by the sea after a big storm. As he walks, he stops and picks up the starfish that have been washed ashore and throws them back into the water.

A passer-by stops and asks: 'Why are you bothering to do that? There are so many that you can never make a difference.'

In reply, the man bends down and picks up another starfish, throws it into the water. 'It made a difference to that one,' he says simply.

No one person can save every homeless animal out there, nor can they stop all the cruelty in the world. What we can do, however, is make small differences. We can choose to adopt a pet rather than buy one; we can volunteer our time to help a shelter or animal welfare organisation and we can teach the world's children that animals need to be treated with respect. If we can't afford anything else, we can still help spread the message and reach those who have the means but might not have even known there was a cause needing support. The important thing to remember is that we should never feel we cannot give enough and therefore there's no point in even trying. If everyone in the world would do just one tiny thing to help animals, the change would be tremendous! The difference we make is felt by each and every individual animal that we save.

Angela was definitely a cat person. I couldn't imagine her reacting in the same way towards a dog. Ask most people and they are likely to dub themselves as either a cat or dog person. Research suggests that our choice of a furry friend says something about who we are. It seems there are differences between cat people and dog people. A University of Texas study found that those who define themselves as dog people are more extrovert, agreeable and conscientious, while those who prefer felines are more adventurous but also prone to be neurotic and anxious. Where a sense of humour is concerned, those who prefer dogs are more likely to enjoy slapstick, while cat lovers may prefer irony and puns. Both groups, however, talk to animals, see themselves as close to nature and are generally optimistic.

SEVENTEEN

Nino's Cats – Laughter and Tears

A day or two into our endeavour, the locals joined in, amazed by the success of the traps I had bought. In spite of our attempts to keep our activities secret, people found their way to the summerhouse, wanting to watch the operations, and we had to shoo them away. Besides the traps I had bought some sets of stacking cages, which allowed three cats to be separately housed one on top of the other, thus saving a lot of space. On the whole, the felines were remarkably quiet and, in the midst of all this coming and going, Frank and Ross calmly carried out their veterinary duties.

The atmosphere was tense with concentration. We felt we had to speak in whispers. On the first day I wondered if I could watch the operations. Elke was already accustomed to this and encouraged me.

'Yes, come on, Jenny,' Frank added. 'If you want to take photographs and document the project, you need to see what it's all about.'

He lifted an anaesthetised cat onto the table and covered its side with a drape. Elke handed him a scalpel.

'Oh, dear!' I muttered and shrank away.

'OK, OK!' Frank murmured. 'You're not about to see a load of blood. Once we used to make a big incision but now it's more like keyhole surgery.'

He was right. I watched his skilful fingers move swiftly and surely and in minutes it was over – with, as he said, very little blood. Elke gently lifted the cat and laid it in a recovery cage. Soon I was an old hand, helping with sterilising the instruments and handing over medication. But many of the female cats were already pregnant and I never got used to the necessary aborting of kittens.

In the Public Gardens I found a beautiful grey tabby, which had obviously been abandoned as she came to me quite readily. I fell for this pretty little thing and was anxious when it came to her turn for the operation. Unable to stay to watch this one, I went outside and stood staring down at Isola Bella without really seeing it. After a while Elke came out of the summerhouse.

'Don't worry, she's fine, Jenny.'

Isola Bella swam back into focus, the bougainvillea seemed a more intense magenta against the blue sky; I felt absurdly happy.

There was tragedy too. One evening, Nino came over from his *trattoria* with a tiny kitten wrapped up in a blanket.

'This cat is sick, I think. Can you do anything for her?'

103

She was a scrap of a thing with milky, newly opened eyes. They stared at me and my heart went out to her. Elke gave me some special milk for kittens and a pipette and I fought to save her, not sleeping for two nights while she lay beside me in her little blanket on the pillow. On the second day I was close to tears. I willed her to live, giving her all my strength. The rest of the world didn't seem to exist – it was just this tiny scrap and me.

Elke left the summerhouse and came over to where I sat.

'Let me take her to the house at Isola Bella, it will be quieter for her there.'

'You'll look after her?' I queried anxiously.

'Of course I will.'

The next day she told me gently that my little kitten had died on the way down and I realised she had wanted to spare me this. Dear Elke! In future, I would remember her wise words: 'You have to be strong if you do this work.'

I quickly realised it was the wrong time of the year to choose for this venture. June in Taormina is a month of intense heat and we worked in conditions sometimes exceeding 40°C (104°F). Elke had brought in fans for the summerhouse but, the moment you stepped outside, the sun burned fiery hot. I dreaded the trips I had to make to the pharmacist, rushing along the Corso under that scorching sun to pick up more sterile gloves and other supplies.

As the days went by, we became increasingly anxious that word was getting round. We were engaged on something that was technically illegal, flouting Sicilian bureaucracy, which involves mountains of paperwork and so-called laws never carried out. For example, the public sector of the veterinary service, ASL, is supposedly responsible for the neutering of feral cats but it does little if anything about it. The Town Hall agrees it is necessary but money always goes somewhere else. To set up as a private vet, as my friend Giulio told me, you must conform to a tome of rules before being issued with a certificate. All this is exacerbated by two unpleasant traits in the Sicilian character: envy and craftiness, a readiness to inform on anything that might be another's success, adding complications to my apparently simple aim of helping the cats. Nevertheless, during my trip, over a hundred cats were neutered and treated successfully with antibiotics and eye creams.

We were terrified that someone would report us to the police and had to be very careful it was only feral cats we neutered. Towards the end of the week we had a drama. Once more Nino came over from the *trattoria*. We had managed to catch and neuter a number of the feral cats he fed outside the restaurant kitchen. Now he brought a large handsome cat and asked for her to be 'done' as well. Was she feral? Oh yes, of course. Frank operated on her that evening and we put her in a carrier to recover. We couldn't understand why Nino was so anxious to have her back.

Later that evening he called us in a panic: the cat didn't seem well.

'Let her rest,' Frank told him.

Nino called again. 'I'm really worried about the cat, I think she's dying. I'm going to call a local vet.'

This was the last thing we wanted. If a private vet believed, at least theoretically, that we were taking money out of his pocket, then we would almost certainly be reported.

'I'll go over and see him,' Frank sighed. He was on the

point of packing up for the day to go back to Elke's house for dinner.

'Guess what?' he said when he came back. 'That cat wasn't feral, it is his wife's cat – she was away for a few days and Nino thought it was a good opportunity to get it neutered. Now she's coming back in a couple of days and he's panicking.'

We were appalled. If anything happened to this favoured feline, there would be trouble.

'Don't worry,' Frank continued. 'There is nothing wrong with that animal, she is just getting over the anaesthetic. Give her another twenty-four hours and she'll be fine.'

He was right and Nino came over, full of apologies and an invitation to eat in his *trattoria* on our last night. We made doubly sure all cats were feral after that.

By the end of our week's work we were worn out, but jubilant, too: all the cats had come through without problem, cats that were now going to have a better quality of life. It was time for a celebration.

Nino stood in the entrance of his restaurant beaming broadly. It was obvious the cat had made a good recovery.

'Welcome, welcome, my friends!' He waved an expansive hand to the long table set out on the terrace. It bristled with wine glasses and cutlery.

'Make yourselves at home.'

The meal began: it was sumptuous, beginning with *antipasto*. In English we call it the 'appetiser course'. For the French it is *hors d'oeuvre*, in Italy it's called the *antipasto*. It can be hot or cold, cooked or raw, a delicious invitation to the feast that is to follow: the smooth texture of a tuna pâté contrasting with the brilliant colours of parsley, lemon slices and olives, marinated with herbs, stuffed olives with a nutty almond or hot spicy filling, or dark purple kalamata olives, all adding their own flavour and colour. The colours, the artful composition, reminded us that it was time for pleasure, relaxation and indulgence.

Glasses were refilled and we tucked in. Then came the first course, my favourite *Pasta alla Norma*, and then fish, simply grilled with lemon and herbs. More wine and a pause before the desserts arrived, the cassata and panna cotta, the ice cream!

A special guest joined us: Dorothea Fritz, the legendary German vet who directs Lega Pro Animale for the sterilisation of cats and dogs in Naples. Dorothea studied in Munich, then worked in Greece before finally arriving in Naples. Visits to the *canili*, the cruel dog shelters provided by the state, left a lasting impression. She saw more than 450 inmates, living skeletons of dogs, who endured a life of sickness and uncontrolled reproduction. Dorothea decided she could not turn her back on this terrible situation. She acquired a plot of land and in 1986 Lega Pro Animale was born. A small woman with cropped grey hair and a lovely smile, the years of combating authorities have honed her into a tough fighter, unafraid to stand up to any authority. She had come to Taormina for a few days and agreed to accompany me on my proposed foray to the town hall.

This is a seventeenth-century building in Corso Umberto, near the Duomo, Taormina's main church. Its pinkish façade, featuring an arched portico and motifs such as a Star of David, resembles something one would expect to see in Venice. Inside, there is luxurious marble inlay and impressive framed windows sporting coats of arms. A cloister, enclosing an impressive flight of marble stairs, brings you to the first floor.

Here, there is the scene of much coming and going, of people standing in the corridor, clasping their *documenti*. They wait to be admitted, glaring at the closed doors. Suddenly, one such door opens and a personage shoots out and off down the stairs, called away on an urgent errand.

'Come back tomorrow!' The mayor's voice floats back to those who wait and shrug: '*Muh!*'

At a desk in one corner a man like the dog Cerberus, Hades' loyal watchdog, guards the entrance to the council chambers. But the conduct of the mayor and the councillors is a constant source of argument along the Corso. Faults in administration, rising rates and taxes, the cost of living… all this is chewed over. The people of Taormina are great talkers and one of their favourite subjects is party politics.

'He's not going to be here,' Cerberus told me when, for the third time, I climbed that magnificent staircase.

'But this is important,' I protested. 'I know Taormina lives by tourism,' I added, trying a different tack. 'You need to sort out the feral animal situation.'

'Why don't you go to the tourist office?' the hell dog shrugged. 'If it is to do with tourism.'

'It is the mayor I need to see. And I have a very prestigious vet arriving in a few days' time. She has asked me to make an appointment.'

By now I was desperate. I knew that Dorothea was only there on a flying visit.

'*Muh!*' said Cerberus.

The following day, as soon as I could take a break from cat catching, I was back at the town hall. Cerberus was deep in conversation with another man and they eyed me disdainfully. I was only a woman, after all.

'You know what I've come about,' I said. 'Surely the mayor can find a few minutes? Several local vets want to attend a meeting too, people like Dottore Grasso.'

'Grasso?'

I nodded.

The men exchanged a look; the visitor murmured something: I had obviously struck a chord. Cerberus rose and went to tap on the illustrious one's door. He disappeared inside. After a moment he returned.

'Monday at 10am,' he said. His tone was begrudging.

I wondered how my cause had been described. The mention of Grasso had obviously turned the tables in my favour but I was a foreigner and naturally suspect. It put me in mind of the phrase *essere sistemata*. Luigi Barzini, the Italian writer who delved deep into the national character, had something to say about this. The Italian people live in constant political chaos, unable to trust government, public institutions or their neighbour. Envy and jealously are rife. To be *sistemata* is to create a protective shield against this precarious life. A safe, secure job, not aspiring to greatness (such as a university degree), not drawing attention to yourself, marrying and having children provides a sense of inner and outer order — in other words, being *sistemata*. Were they fearful I was trying to disturb this comfortable, if deaf and blind, existence?

Frank returned to America and Elke and I cleared out the

summerhouse. The following day, I met up with Dorothea and we descended on the town hall for our meeting with the local dignitaries.

The mayor, the vice mayor and about a dozen Sicilian vets were assembled in one of the chambers to greet us.

'So, what is all this about?' the mayor demanded. 'Are you animal activists?'

I felt Dorothea stiffen. She had obviously been accused of this before. Her voice was firm, her tone cool.

'Spaying and neutering of stray cats in Italy should be performed free of charge by the public veterinary services, but very often this service does not work well or the numbers neutered are not high enough to make a difference in the territory. We should not forget that a cat at five months of age can already be pregnant and there can be up to four litters in just one year. On average there are three kittens in a litter, but we have found cats pregnant with ten kittens.'

Ten! A collective gasp went round the chamber. This was news to the councillors and maybe the vets too.

'And where do you stand in all this?' the mayor wanted to know.

'I want to stress to you how vital it is to have a proper programme for neutering feral animals,' Dorothea continued. 'If they are left to breed in this way, they suffer and people employ other, more cruel methods of control. In the years I have lived in Naples we have established a spay/neuter clinic and it has made a real difference. If a place to operate could be provided in Taormina, we could initiate a similar project here.'

'I don't see why not,' observed the mayor. 'It seems like

a good idea. I should think we could provide such a place somewhere in the town.'

He turned to confer with the others, who nodded their heads and murmured agreement. I noted a surreptitious glancing at watches – were they thinking about lunch? It certainly appeared our time was up; our hands were shaken and we found ourselves once more out in the blazing hot Corso Umberto.

'What do you think?' I asked Dorothea. 'They did seem to listen to you.'

But Dorothea gave an expressive shrug. 'Words are easy. Whether they will actually do anything is another story. The moment it becomes a question of money they'll find a hundred other things that are more important.'

I was silent in the face of such cynicism. A few minutes ago I had really believed the assembly had seen reason and Catsnip would be able to operate on a more legal basis. It was going to take some time before I arrived at Dorothea's resignation to this inherent apathy, one that has been voiced so well in the novel *The Leopard*: 'Sleep, my dear Chevalley, eternal sleep, that is what Sicilians want. And they will always resent anyone who tries to awaken them, even to bring them the most wonderful of gifts'.

EIGHTEEN

Genoveffa, the Little Cat Lady with a Big Heart

*T*he heat intensified. Throughout that July of 2003, I visited the various cat colonies in the town. I had two aims: to treat cats with antibiotics and, more specifically, an eye cream for a particularly vicious ailment that, left untreated, results in the cats going blind, and to make friends with the *gattare*, those wonderful cat ladies who take it upon themselves to feed a colony of cats. In this way I met Genoveffa.

Towards the end of the Corso, gazing out towards Etna, is the pastel pink building of Pensione Adele with its white balustrades; it always reminded me of a huge pink and white iced cake. Once a palazzo, it had been turned into a hotel. In a courtyard at the back I had seen a small colony of cats. Now it was time to meet their *gattara*.

I rang on the bell and the door clicked open, letting me into a cavernous hallway at the foot of a wide, curving staircase. As I looked upwards, I saw Genoveffa's smiling face gazing down at me.

'Come on up!'

The high-ceilinged breakfast room was furnished with the traditional Sicilian furniture and chandeliers.

'*Vuole un caffe?*'

'Thank you, but...'

'I know!' Genoveffa nodded and smiled. 'I'll make you a *cappuccino*. I have so many foreigners here, every year – I should know their tastes by now.'

I sat down in an armchair and, leaning my head against the lace-edged antimacassar, I told Genoveffa about my plans for the future. As long as I could find somewhere to operate, I intended to return the following year for another neutering session to try to control the feral cat population.

Genoveffa might have been small and slight but I found in this woman a passionate supporter of cats, angered by the attitude of people in the neighbourhood. She welcomed my plan and thanked me for trying to help.

'Come and meet my cats.'

We went through to the storeroom, where there was a big stack of cat food, and then out into the yard to see her colony. They were a strange little group: one with half a tail, another who limped – victims of the cars that swung into the parking space behind the hotel, drivers caring only to find a space. I mentioned to one or two of them they should be careful but they just shrugged. Genoveffa spoke to the cats by name and they rubbed themselves against her legs.

She told me about the object she found that she thought was meat wrapped in newspaper only to discover to her horror it was a dead cat.

'They have no heart,' she said.

Pensione Adele was founded in 1957 by the Cascio family, around the time of the golden age of mass tourism. A different breed of visitor began to arrive in Taormina, where once wealthy independent travellers had spent the winter months. The Adele offered clean, spacious rooms and warm hospitality at a reasonable price.

Over the next few years I often visited Genoveffa. She was always an oasis of kindness and understanding while I struggled to help the cats.

NINETEEN

The Tale of Ginger and Lucky Star

*C*atsnip was not even a year old but was already establishing a name as a resource for cat welfare. I set up a website and wrote of our first neutering week. There was an unexpected result: I found myself becoming an advice centre. Tourists visiting the island would be concerned about an animal and go online, where it appeared I was almost the only point of contact. I received emails asking how cats would survive in winter when hotels closed, reports of chained dogs spotted in small villages on the side of Mount Etna, looking half-starved and ill. One couple called me, concerned about a small cat they had seen, which they had called Ginger.

'She's hardly more than a kitten,' Terry told me. 'We've been going to their colony to feed them every day and we're worried about her. She seems to have something wrong with her eyes. Is there anything we can do?'

I knew very well what they were talking about, the problem that shows itself as conjunctivitis but is often linked to upper respiratory infection, common among cats and kittens in Sicily.

'Go to the pharmacist in the Corso,' I advised, 'and buy a tube of Pensulvit.'

'The pharmacist?' Terry sounded surprised.

'Oh yes, they sell products for animals, too.' I told him. I knew that because I had marvelled myself when I bought my first tube.

Obviously they took my advice. On my next trip to Taormina I went in search of her, clasping a photograph Terry had sent me. It took me a while to identify her neighbourhood, wandering in the small streets below the Corso. But then a small and seemingly fragile cat came running towards me, unmistakably Ginger!

I met up with Terry and Natalya when they came to Brighton to show me a sheaf of photographs of their beloved Ginger. She now appeared to be thriving and already they were planning their next visit to see her.

Over the next two years the continuing story of Ginger unfolded. Terry and Natalya returned several times to Taormina, their principal aim, apart from sunning themselves by the hotel pool and enjoying good food in the evenings, being to check on Ginger. We all agreed that she (ginger cats are usually male, but this Ginger was female) should be neutered.

The stumbling block was a local *gattara* who fed her; Marika put her foot down. She was afraid the cat would die under anaesthetic.

'You'll have to get her on your side,' I advised them. 'You can't just ride roughshod over her wishes. After all, she feeds Ginger all year round, while you are only there for a week or so.'

So the neutering of Ginger was delayed and another year passed. One morning, I checked on my emails and saw that Terry and Natalya were back in Taormina once again. I expected to have a good progress report but Terry sounded concerned: Ginger was very poorly and her body was covered in what looked like scabs, which she was continually scratching. I suggested they contact Oscar La Manna, my wonderful local vet, who concerns himself with the plight of feral animals, and ask him to come and take a look at her.

'He says it's mushrooms,' they wrote later.

Mushrooms! I puzzled over this for a while and then remembered the raised rings on my sister's skin and mine when we were children, infected by various family cats. It was ringworm, of course, caused by a fungus that grows on the skin like a mushroom on the bark of a tree. I had to laugh.

'She is being treated but he also wants to neuter her. Apparently, she's had several litters of kittens that have all died and he thinks it for the best.'

It was arranged that Oscar La Manna would return the following morning, but when Terry and Natalya arrived they found that Ginger had beaten everyone to it. Overnight she had given birth to kittens and tucked them all away in an inaccessible place.

As Oscar said: 'I can't treat her while she is feeding the kittens and she will have to stay where she is.'

Sadly, Ginger's kittens died but it meant the treatment could be started.

Marika agreed to talk to the couple when they explained, 'We don't want Ginger to go through this experience again. It's kinder to have her neutered.'

This time, the *gattara* agreed.

Another case of 'touristitis', as my friend Kathy described it. She lives in the north of Italy, Trieste, where sentiments towards animals are very different. Terry and Natalya were typical of so many British and Northern European visitors who find it difficult to understand the locals' attitude towards animals.

Lucky Star was indeed the most fortunate of kittens. Local people in Taormina wonder at Laura, the young woman who never takes a holiday but chooses to spend her time and money caring for cats. Even her doting father feels that her attitude might be a bit exaggerated.

'It's fine to love cats,' he says. 'But I'm concerned by how much stress it gives her.'

Nevertheless, every ten days or so, the two of them drove to an out-of-town supermarket, where Laura stocked up on cut-price tins and packets of cat food. Taormina, as I've said before, is beautiful – indeed, the guidebooks class it as one of the loveliest places in the world. The Public Gardens are an oasis of calm, where the tourist can stroll among palm trees along shady paths, dreaming green thoughts. Laura knows differently, though: she has glimpsed the dark side of this perfect little town. She understands only too well the violence, the indifference of its inhabitants, and the reality of this so-called corner of Paradise.

'Come and see my cats,' she invited.

I followed her down uneven stone steps away from the main street with its boutique shops and pavement cafes – the throng of visitors taking a walk after the heat of the day had cooled. We walked along a narrow street where several motorbikes were parked against a row of garages. And there they were: her cats, the colony she fed and cared for… ginger, black, white, black and white and tabby, all meowing and pressing their bodies against Laura's legs. Each of them had a name.

'That's Marchetto, here is Bianca and this is Nino,' she told me.

The black cat had a healing wound across the top of his head. He was wary of me and wouldn't come near.

'Someone hit him,' Laura explained, 'some imbecile. Nino disappeared for several days and came back with this awful cut across his head. I rushed him to the vet and, thank God, he is recovering.'

Just as she was filling plastic bowls with cat food, a door shot open and a woman came towards us. She was furious.

'Stop that! Just stop that! If you want to feed these miserable creatures take them to your house and do it there.'

She aimed a kick at one of the bowls, but Laura stepped in her way.

'If you continue doing this,' the woman hissed, 'I shall report you to the police.'

Laura did not reply and, after a while, the woman retreated to her house.

'She can't touch me,' said Laura. 'People are always threatening me but there is no law that forbids feeding these cats.

'It is the hatred of these people towards animals that upsets me,' she continued, as we climbed the steps again and joined the crowds in the main street. 'They treat them like vermin. There's been a spate of poisoning, but of course we never know who has done it and so we can't report them.'

The light was fading. Tourists gathered in Piazza IX Aprile, the huge main square, to lean on the railings and gaze towards the twinkling lights along the coast, the illuminated Greek Theatre. The scent of jasmine intensified. Children chased each other or crowded round the ice-cream cart. It was a scene of such tranquillity; incongruous with the landscape Laura was painting. This place began to seem like a theatrical illusion of light, colour and laughter concealing a sordid truth. Now that I understood Laura's 'reality', it all seemed flimsy and somewhat corrupt.

'There used to be so many cats here,' Laura said, as we strolled among the roses and lilies of the Public Gardens. 'Now there are very few; it's certain someone is poisoning them.'

We came across one of the gardeners humming under his breath as he watered a yellow hibiscus. The sun shone through the stream of water creating a miniature rainbow – he seemed happy to be caring for this garden.

'Where are the ginger kittens?' Laura called out 'I can't see them anywhere.'

As he glanced up, we could see his mood change. He shrugged and then went back to his work.

'You see, they really don't care,' said Laura.

A few days later I went in search of Laura and found she was very upset. Someone had put four kittens into a bag and literally thrown them away in a rubbish bin. Animal-loving friends of Laura noticed a faint meowing and rescued them. They were tiny; probably born only a couple of days ago. Two were dead but the others were blindly searching for food. Their crying was breaking Laura's heart.

Together we went to the pharmacist to buy the special milk for kittens and a small pipette. It is an onerous task rearing newborn felines – they need to be fed every two or three hours.

'I don't know how we'll manage,' Laura confessed. 'I'm working all day and my father certainly wouldn't allow me to nurse kittens in his shop.'

Fortunately her friends, the couple who had found the kittens, said they would take responsibility.

Once again I was struck by the juxtaposition of peace and violence in this place. Here was a cafe where people laughed and were tipsy on sun and wine, without a care in the world. I wanted to tell them that a few yards away from this jolly scene there was a pile of rubbish where some cruel individual, having snatched those mites from their mother, had dumped them here.

I was reminded of W.H. Auden's poem 'Musee des Beaux Arts' and of how suffering takes place in the midst of ordinary, careless life.

Auden visited the Museum of Fine Arts in Brussels in 1938 and viewed *Icarus Falling* by Bruegel. The theme of his poem is the apathy with which humans view individual suffering. You might say Breugel's painting doesn't take it that seriously – if you look closer at the untroubled ship sailing by, you can see the foolish and drowning son of Dedalus, legs akimbo, sticking out of the water. Is the artist trying to say that life is absurd, suffering insignificant? Or was it meant to portray the Icarus event as being of no consequence in order to strengthen the point of the painting?

Would these happy travellers be shocked by what I told them, or would they resent that I had disturbed the calm surface of their stay? I wondered.

Laura told me that one of the kittens had died but the other one was fighting on; however, there was a new problem. Her friends were going on holiday, one that was booked months ago. What was to happen to the kitten? Would violence win after all?

She got out her contact book and we phoned around. A cat lover in a neighbouring village apologised profusely; she had to take her ailing husband to hospital. We sent emails to others but no one bothered to reply.

The best way forward was to pay a vet but the first, a truly caring man, was up to his eyeballs in work and could not take anything more on, he told us.

Meanwhile, the day was fast approaching when Laura's friends would depart. I was also on the verge of leaving for England. Laura was becoming desperate: if this tiny scrap of life wasn't fed, she would die. Laura was in tears.

And then the small miracle occurred: another vet didn't hesitate. 'Yes, I will take the kitten. There is a young and newly qualified vet in the surgery. She is willing to help and I will be in attendance to keep my eye on things.'

Time passed and the tiny feline thrived. She eats like 'a little pig', Laura told me, 'she purrs, she plays – there are some people in this apathetic world who aren't indifferent to animal suffering.'

Laura drove to the surgery to see her. She was now a ball of white, with smudges of grey fluff. It was clear the young woman vet had fallen in love with her. The kitten's miserable past was forgotten and there was no self-pity.

As another poet, D.H. Lawrence, observed, he 'never saw a wild thing sorry for itself'. Lawrence lived for nearly three years in this place, a tortured soul forever wandering, but who found a degree of harmony here.

On my return, Laura took me to see the kitten. Back with the animal-loving friends, she would soon be adopted into a loving home. Scuttling about our feet, she played with my shoelace and then, like all young things, she suddenly tired. She curled into a ball and went to sleep... and slept with such tranquillity. All was well.

'What will you call her?' I asked.

While Laura considered, I looked back over these days and the undertones of cruelty and violence I had witnessed. Certainly there was sunshine here but also a world of shadows.

Laura had been watching as the kitten woke, yawned and immediately settled off to sleep again.

'*Stella Fortunata*,' she said at last.

I translated the words to English: 'Lucky Star'.

Oblivious, the kitten slept on. Suddenly, all the questions and imponderables faded and I felt myself in the moment, rejoicing that one small being had been saved. I am not religious in the accepted sense, although I have my own beliefs, but now the words of the hymn 'Amazing Grace' brought tears to my eyes: 'I once was lost and now am found...'

I smiled at Laura.

'Oh yes, let's call her Lucky Star!'

TWENTY

A Crash Course in the Sicilian Psyche

For the attention of the Mayor: Dear Sir, following our visit to the town hall in June of this year when you agreed to provide a room for the neutering and treatment of feral cats can you confirm that this will be made available?

Sir, please can you reply to my email of October?

I am presently planning my next visit to Taormina to carry out more work with the feral cats. Can you please let me know how arrangements have proceeded for the provision of facilities?

Silence. I did not hear another word.

'Words are easy,' Dorothea Fritz had said. 'It's whether they actually do something about it.'

How right she had been. As so often, I turned back to *The Leopard*: 'It doesn't matter about doing things well or badly; the sin which we Sicilians never forgive is simply that of "doing" at all. It's not a case of universal apathy: the people who try to do things are invariably checked by those who don't'.

But I was not prepared to give up. Throughout the winter of 2003 I continued to raise funds and to campaign for the free movement of foreign vets within EEC countries. I even lobbied then Prime Minister Silvio Berlusconi!

Susan Dale from the Anglo-Italian Society for the Protection of Animals listened to my woes with a sympathetic ear.

'I wondered if it would be possible for Dorothea Fritz to bring her mobile ambulance from Naples,' I ventured. 'I could pay expenses.'

'That would be a way forward. I'll talk to Dorothea and see how she is fixed.'

So I called Elke.

'That's wonderful news but where are we to operate?'

We had decided it was too risky to use the summerhouse again. Nino's panic over his wife's cat, the way word had spread round Taormina in spite of our attempts at secrecy, had more or less put paid to that.

'Well, if Taormina isn't interested,' she said, 'I'll talk to the Mayor of Letojanni. I'm on good terms with him.'

She was true to her word and a week later called me to say he had agreed to allow Dorothea's spaymobile to be parked in a large garage in the little town. Not only that, he offered Dorothea and her two colleagues free board in an apartment and meals in local restaurants. Catsnip could spring into action again!

I left England on 4 May 2004. My plan was to spend the two weeks prior to Dorothea's arrival spreading the news of our programme among the local people and locating colonies of cats.

Letojanni is only a short bus ride away but a very different tourist venue from Taormina. Situated on the coast, it has wide shingle beaches, unlike the bay of Isola Bella. It has, in my view, the normal atmosphere of a community going about its business, although tourism is steadily on the increase. At one time it was just a small fishing village. When the railway line and the main road were established in 1866, Letojanni became increasingly important and many influential families moved down from the mountains of Gallodoro to take up residence there. One of these was the Durante family and Francesco Durante was to become a famous 'son'. His father wanted him to study engineering but Fate took a hand the day he visited the Messina University of Medicine with a friend who was studying there. Amazed at Durante's comments and obvious scientific bent, a professor urged him to study medicine and he became an outstanding student. Later, the young Durante moved to Rome where, in 1872, he conceived and founded a general hospital. When Messina was devastated by the terrible earthquake of 1908, Durante was there with medical supplies, working with a group of volunteers to create field hospitals. Sicily had called him back as it does so many of its countrymen. His accomplishments were honoured in 1923 when the 'poor' of Letojanni erected a monument, a bronze bust by Ettore

Ximenes, celebrated Palermitan sculptor, in what is now called Piazza Durante.

Whenever I stroll in this square I am startled by its grandeur: wide, light and airy and fringed by tall palm trees, it seems as if a giant hand has plucked it from a far larger city and dropped it down here. Bars and cafes surround it, including the Niny bar, famed for its granita and delicious ice cream. When it became too hot to continue my ramblings round the village, I'd sit at one of the outside tables under a huge white umbrella and spoon up the coffee ice crystals topped with whipped cream; served with a brioche it is a favourite summer breakfast among Sicilians. I'd watch the to-ing and fro-ing across this beautiful piazza. On one of these occasions I was intrigued by a tall, dark-haired figure clasping a black document folder, who strode with such presence I was sure he must be a person of some importance, an actor perhaps. Later, I was to discover my guess had not been far from the truth.

After some delay, Elke had managed to secure the prized *permesso*, the official document from the town hall permitting our team to carry out their work with feral cats. This time, there was no need for secrecy or fear of the dreaded *denuncia*. It's a threat you often hear in Sicily: 'I'm going to make a *denuncia* to the police,' an irate housewife will say as you spoon Whiskas onto a plastic plate in the street. The *denuncia* had been a very real threat during our Taormina episode but there was no fear of that this time. Now, I could go public. I contacted a journalist who worked for *La Sicilia*, who found it an interesting human interest story – a change from the usual daily diet of politics and sport. He invited me to his house in Letojanni and photographed me holding an unwilling cat.

On 23 May, Dorothea, together with Naples vet Anna Maria and cat catcher supreme Teresa, travelled on the night ferry from Naples to Catania. Elke and I waited by the garage to greet them. And there they came, driving in convoy along the road that ran by the sea, the spaymobile followed by a large van. People stopped to stare. Letojanni had never seen anything like this before. By the time they reached the garage there was quite a crowd, curious to know what was going on. Calmly, Dorothea and her team set about unloading cages and traps, more than I had seen so far. They obviously meant business. We organised ourselves in the garage, which housed the two vehicles easily enough with plenty of space around them to set out the cages. Emilia from the Palm Beach Cafe on the other side of the piazza appeared bearing a tray.

'I thought you could do with some coffee,' she said.

You could see she too was curious to find out what was going on. Her eyes widened at the sight of so many traps. Dorothea drank her coffee swiftly while she darted questions at Elke and me. What area were we covering? Were there any local people willing to help? No, she wouldn't stop for lunch.

We're in for a tough week, I told myself.

Soon Teresa and I set off on the first of our many cat-catching trips.

Feral cats are very crafty. Several entered a trap and delicately ate the bait while managing not to put a paw on the spring mechanism. We also saw several mother cats pick up and carry away their almost grown-up kittens in their mouths. It was incredible how they seemed to intuit what was going on! Nevertheless, we caught enough to keep Dorothea and Anna Maria working from early in the morning till mid-evening with scarcely a stop for lunch.

'They must eat something,' Emilia protested when she heard Dorothea had decided not to go to the restaurant for lunch.

She packed up large *panini* stuffed with cheese, ham and tomato and sent them over to the garage, where we perched on boxes in the sunshine to eat and relax for half an hour. But it was always only half an hour. I learned a lot from Dorothea, who worked with German efficiency. Her years in Naples struggling with cruelty and the plight of sickly animals had given her a steely resolve, which sometimes made me feel ineffectual. I was still a novice with all the idealism that implied and had a lot of toughening up to do. Even though I knew we were doing it in their best interests, I was finding the capture of these cats an increasingly stressful experience. My heart went out to their cries and frantic attempts to escape and I was always relieved when the time came to release them again.

Every cat we caught was put in a labelled cage ensuring they would return to their own colony. The vets also tattooed each feline to indicate it had been neutered. Only one cat had to be put to sleep; he had an ulcerated tumour in the mouth and was incapable of eating or drinking. All the others (seventy female and forty-five male) recovered well.

Thanks to the local cat ladies, most of the cats were quite well fed but they did suffer from fleas, ticks and worms, which had to be treated. Cats with respiratory symptoms were given long-action antibiotics and eye drops. Follow-up treatment is impossible; these animals are used to being free so that keeping them in cages any longer than is necessary for recovery from their operations constitutes maltreatment.

Early on in the week a couple turned up at the garage. Cheery-faced Maria Annunciata and her tall German husband Norbert had heard about the spaymobile and were curious to see what was going on.

'We've heard so much about you and the wonderful work you are doing. But what made you come to Letojanni?' Maria wanted to know.

Dorothea, busy as always and bent over an inert cat, jerked her head in my direction, where I was checking on some of the sleeping cats.

'Thank you, thank you so much!' Maria enthused. '*Mamma mia*, what a wonderful thing to be doing!'

'We'd better go outside,' I said, not wishing to disturb the vets' concentration.

'We'd really like to help you, wouldn't we, Norbert?' Maria continued. 'What can we do?'

'Please, help me find some more cats.'

I was feeling a bit desperate. At the rate Dorothea and Anna Maria were working, we would soon run out. I knew what that meant: with nothing to do, she would pack up early and leave. There was no messing about with Dorothea.

So we spread ourselves wider, Maria and Norbert taking me to parts of Letojanni I had never visited before. These were areas of larger houses with big gardens and plenty of cats. Anxious to keep Dorothea supplied, I trespassed without scruples, wandering among lemon and orange trees, stalking felines. I was down on my hands and knees crawling in someone's shrubbery when I heard a voice demand: 'Who's there?' When I emerged with my hair awry and my face streaming with sweat, it took some explaining as to what exactly I was doing there.

On another day a skinny young man in a yellow council jacket turned up in the garage. He hung around the ambulance, fascinated by the two vets at work. The following day he was back. Dorothea seemed to appreciate Alfio's intelligent questions and didn't turn him away.

'I'd really love to have been a vet,' he told her, 'but I left school when I was fifteen and started work.'

Alfio was probably in his twenties but his features seemed to belong to another era: a narrow face with a high forehead and dark hair slicked back. He worked as a refuse collector, which seemed to be a job that gave him quite a lot of the day to himself. Dorothea soon enlisted his help and he proved to be a tireless worker, learning quickly what to do. He helped us carry the cats in their cages to and from their colonies and watched, fascinated, over them as they emerged from their anaesthetic.

'She's woken up!' he would call triumphantly. 'She's fine.'

I think he would have made a good vet.

It was an exhilarating feeling: Letojanni was rallying round. My journalist friend couldn't keep away. He kept on turning up at the garage to interview us and we were featured in *La Sicilia* at least three times during that week.

Teresa was a true Neapolitan with the classic looks of an Old Master and a loud, infectious chuckle. As we drove around the countryside on our cat search we became good friends. One day we were walking past some ramshackle, empty houses when Teresa suddenly stopped.

'Shh, listen!'

It was the sound of a puppy whining but we couldn't make out where it was coming from. We retraced our steps until we came to a house where the lower panels of the door were missing. Teresa went down on her haunches.

'It's in there,' she muttered and clambered through the hole. Soon she reappeared and handed up a small white puppy. It was shivering and whimpering.

'What was it doing in there?' I asked.

'I don't know, but it's too young to fend for itself. It's coming with us!'

'What shall we call her?' Teresa asked as we drove back to the garage.

I mused that the little dog had somehow restored my belief in what I was doing. We were there to help animals live a better life and that would certainly ring true for this one. Teresa had already said she was going to take her home to Naples.

'What about Speranza?' I suggested. 'Hope, in English.'

'I like it. That's what we'll call her.'

It's good to know that little Hope is now in Naples having a great life with Teresa's other dogs.

When we began to run out of cats, Elke came to the rescue again, this time taking us further afield to the area around Mazzaro Bay, below Taormina. We drove up into town to catch some of Genoveffa's colony. She was waiting outside her kitchen and, as we approached, put her finger to her lips and beckoned us inside.

'Thank you for coming but we have to be careful. There is a neighbour who is spying on me and if she sees us with the trap she'll go to the police.'

The *permesso* extended only as far as the borders of Letojanni so we had to take care no one saw us. We sat in the *salotta* while Genoveffa hovered in the yard, watching the neighbour's movements. After about half an hour she came in, smiling.

'I've just seen her go out with her shopping bags. Hurry before she comes back!'

As I have said before, cats take their time but we were able to catch three of them and stow them away in the car before the suspicious neighbour returned.

By early afternoon on the Friday we had to admit defeat; we could find no more cats. For the first time that week we could sit down to a meal at a respectable hour rather than nine or ten at night. We went to Ciao Ciao, my favourite eatery in Letojanni, set right on the beach. It was a wonderfully warm night and we could hear the soft sough of the waves breaking and watch the moon laying its silver path across the water. As all the tensions of the week melted away I realised I was ravenous. I ordered and devoured a huge pizza Siciliana. It was loaded with capers and anchovies and I knew from past experience I would pay for it with a great thirst later on but I can never resist this dish. The others dug into their pasta and pizza, and the wine jug was refilled. With the voices of local people in my ears, on this perfect night I felt at peace with the world. We stayed late, chatting and laughing, high on the success of our amazing week.

The following day the ambulance and van were packed

up ready to leave. In those few days the intensity and accomplishments of our work had drawn us close together; we hugged and kissed and a few tears were shed.

Before I left for England once again I discovered the identity of the figure I'd watched strolling in Piazza Durante. His name is Mario and he has acted and directed in the theatre for many years of his life. I was talking to the man in Letojanni's Internet shop when Mario came over to join us. He seemed delighted to find someone who spoke English and we went for a coffee.

'I'm sorry, it's time to leave,' I said.

Mario smiled. 'You'll be back.'

And 2005 had scarcely begun before I was indeed back in Taormina. I really should have learned by now that proposals by Sicilian authorities are delusive as will o' the wisp, offering false hope, which is never fulfilled. Nevertheless, there I was in chilly January, staying in a damp apartment and awaiting summons to the city of Messina for a meeting with Sicilian vets. And waiting; I called Mario and caught the bus to Letojanni. We met for tea at Il Gabbiano cafe. I was curious to know why he continued to live in this small village where he obviously didn't belong spiritually, among people who didn't understand him.

'You understand, dear Jenny? It seems I might be an agent of the British Secret Service!' He noticed my quizzical expression. 'I mean it, that is how they see me here in Letojanni.'

But I didn't know whether he was joking or not. I glanced down at the black and white photographs scattered over the cafe table: Mario's theatrical history, the plays he'd acted in all over Europe, taking him further and further from his Sicilian roots into the world of Brecht, Theatre of Cruelty, Theatre of the Absurd. There were some reviews written in English spanning the nine years he lived in London.

As he had explained to me during this short winter's afternoon, that was his most serious false step. He went against his better judgement to move from Rome to Norwood, where there was nothing to do in the evenings but go to the pub – his reason: a summer affair with an Englishwoman, which was prolonged because she found herself pregnant.

'The moment she was back in England, she changed. She went back to her work as a lecturer and I was left floundering, a fish out of water. I stayed for the sake of my daughter – until she was old enough to understand. Then we separated but, you understand, I'd lost all my theatrical contacts.'

Now he was 'exiled' in Sicily, in what he called a miserable trap. It was nearly a year since I'd met him in the Internet shop, checking his emails as if it were a lifeline.

I thought of the figure I saw striding towards me as I sat waiting outside Il Gabbiano, enjoying the winter sunshine. He had swept along the street, his long, dark overcoat flapping, dark glasses, film-star good looks. Mario was tall and handsome in a slightly sinister way. His eyes were dark and intent, his smile wry. He had the most wonderful gravelly voice and spoke Italian beautifully. More indefinably he had the elegance of another age; his manners were delightful. You could imagine Mario belonging to some Mittle-europe cafe society seated in one of those Grande Caffes you see in Turin, his constant companions wickedly dark coffee and a smouldering cigarette. Come to think of it...

'Well, you do look rather like a secret agent,' I said.

Mario laughed and shook his head. He refilled our cups. I stared at the translucent liquid with a momentary longing for a comforting English brew, something to warm me. The conversation on the bus as I rode to and from Taormina for these teatime rendezvous with Mario centred on the normally Anglo-Saxon subject of weather. No one had ever known Sicily to be as cold as it was this January. The elderly woman muffled from head to toe in coat and scarves leaned over to offer the driver a sweet, speaking in a high keening voice about '*il freddo*'. And he – taking one hand off the wheel to accept it – commiserated: '*Da fa morire.*' (I smiled to myself. Enough to kill you. Hardly!)

'Come on!' I wanted to say. 'It's not *that* bad. Look out the window, see the sun on the sea, you're not snow-bound like North Italy.' We were swinging down the curving roads towards Letojanni, past stone walls covered with bougainvillea. 'Cold? What kind of blood have you got in your veins?'

The driver's mobile phone rang and he answered. A friend, it seemed, who wanted to meet up that evening. '*Dependere del tempo* (It depends on the weather),' he sighed.

I knew about the truly freezing weather in northern Italy because I'd been watching the RAI news every night, sitting in my damp apartment with a glass of red wine. I was grateful I'd brought warm pyjamas and a hot water bottle with me.

Taormina was dead at this time of year; the bars closed at 20.30, a few people scuttling along the empty streets like crabs on the bottom of the ocean. There was nothing to do but go back to the apartment, eat and watch television until it was time for bed.

I can't see you doing this fifteen years ago, I told myself. *If you were tucked up cosily in bed then, it would be a matrimoniale, a huge double bed, with a Sicilian lover.* Certainly not cuddling a hot water bottle in my narrow, not very comfortable bed, which must stand away from the wall because of the damp. Surreal.

Several times over these last two weeks I'd asked myself, *What am I doing here?* although I knew the answer. I was awaiting a meeting with the head of veterinary services in Messina – a meeting that should have happened the week I arrived.

'Pazienza,' Sergio, president of the National Canine Defence League (Taormina branch), told me. 'The boss is very busy, he has people coming to see him every day.'

'Doesn't he know that I've come all the way from England to see him?' I complained.

Sergio gave an expressive Sicilian shrug: '*Muh!*'

I was trying to be patient because there was so much at stake. The meeting was to discuss the necessity for a permanent clinic for feral cats in Taormina. If I succeeded with this, the next part of my plan, it would be an enormous breakthrough in what had otherwise become a gridlock situation. But on nights like these, watching people in Milan and Turin struggling through snow, hearing a kidnapped Italian journalist pleading for her life, I lost heart. That's why I escaped to Letojanni to have tea with Mario, when we could at least commiserate together.

Every time we entered Il Gabbiano, heads turned. I knew they were trying to work out whether we slept together – indeed, why we were together at all. Already they'd found this lengthy stay of Mario's mysterious and then he turns up with a foreign woman – just what was going on? I imagined them asking each other as they turned back to their tables and leaned their heads together.

What they didn't know was that we were linked by a common sense of exile, a kind of existential waiting. I, the meeting in Messina; Mario, confirmation of a drama workshop he had proposed at nearby Roccalumera. If he didn't do something concrete, he said, he would go mad.

But with Mario there was a mutual reticence, a tacit understanding that our conspiracy should remain at this cerebral level. Hard to explain, a sense I didn't understand myself: taboo. Of course, I had had my initial fantasies – I wouldn't be Jenny if I hadn't. But there was an actor's narcissism about him, which warned me that any involvement would be a disaster. A complicity of *attente* then but we were both aware that it was probable nothing might occur. This was Sicilianita as the author of *The Leopard*, Tomasi di Lampedusa, confirmed in the voice of the Prince of Salina:

The Sicilians never want to improve for the simple reason that they think themselves perfect; their vanity is stronger than their misery; every invasion by outsiders, whether so by origin or, if Sicilian, by independence of spirit, upsets their illusion of achieved perfection, risks disturbing their satisfied waiting for nothing.

Mario passed me the plate of *dolce* and I took a *cannoli* – a kind of cream horn. Then I regretted it because they are squishy things to eat.

'Here you are watched and checked every day, whom you frequent, where you take your coffee, with what linguistic vocabulary you express yourself, who you are, politically based on country and tribal; politics and so on. It's tragic and grotesque.'

And I was right – a *cannoli* is not something you eat in public. I wiped my fingers, took a sip of tea.

'And that's without mentioning their penchant for destruction and self-destruction, their gratuitous slander,' Mario commented.

It was all too much. We could not stay here, he said. We must move on somewhere else. I stood at the counter waiting while he paid, conscious of the eyes boring into my back, following us as we left the cafe. Outside, I zipped up my jacket. A chilly wind blew through the deserted Piazza Durante. The leaves of the palm trees rustled mournfully. We crossed swiftly and pushed open the door to the Pegasus bar (sadly no more). It was the haunt of the intelligentsia or what passes for intelligentsia in Letojanni. I'd had some heated discussions on the meaning of life in here, sitting round a table and eating their special *bruschetta*, which are nothing like the ubiquitous toast with a bit of chopped tomato and onion on top. The Pegasus *bruschetta* were chunky laden affairs and the red wine to wash them down not the often watery variety, which I suspected came from the cartons you can buy in the supermarket for seventy pence.

Tonight Fabrizio was here, just arrived from Florence, where he now lived. 'It's good to come back to Sicily,' he told me, 'but only for two or three weeks.' You got the impression that, if, by mistake, he stayed longer, his re-entry into Florence would somehow be mysteriously refused. Now and again, Mario disappeared outside to stand in the cold night air and smoke. He was an inveterate smoker, although some days he told me he had given up. I understood. There was a time when I couldn't write a word without a cup of coffee and a cigarette. What I found extraordinary was that somehow the smoking ban was observed. Since the beginning of that year it had become forbidden to smoke in restaurants, bars and cafes, forbidden with draconian force – alien to the usual laissez-faire attitude of this country.

Mario returned to take up where he had left off.

'So I am a British secret agent, huh! The only thing you can do with people like these is to have a good laugh. That's if you don't shudder at how it's linked with serious psychological problems mixed with ignorance, lack of common sense and petty provincial imaginings…'

Peppe behind the counter caught my eye and shrugged.

'…The deadly boredom of a subculture, of suspicion, frustration and mortal apathy.'

He was right, of course, I thought, remembering the time when I lived briefly with Amadeo. By the end of the day 'someone' would have told him my precise movements: that I'd taken a stroll in the Public Gardens, where I'd been spotted talking to an old man. In the market I had again spoken to an elderly stallholder for what seemed like a suspiciously long time and then I'd sat in the Oranges Bar with a glass of wine in the middle of the day!

Every Sicilian is an island within the family or group of those who directly surround him. He can be courageous, generous and fearless. On the dark side he is also capable of dealing death in a real or metaphorical way if he thinks it is necessary. His intelligence is often interpreted as *furbizia* or cunning. '*Fatti furbo*,' you will hear a father call after his son as he leaves the house. ('Don't let anyone get one over you.') It is no insult to call someone '*furbo*'. It means that, whereas most people accomplish a simple project with a chat over a drink, or a letter, to a Sicilian it becomes an undertaking of Promethean proportions. Each side will be involved in cooking up a wicked scheme to get the better of the other while trying to foresee the schemes the other might invent; in fact, being even more *furbo*. The result is very often stalemate, the paralysis of two equally talented chess players, the 'feeling of death' described by Lampedusa.

It was that kind of stalemate I was facing now: every move I made was checked by the authorities as 'not legal', coupled by the vice of '*domani, domani*' – always tomorrow.

As I remarked to Mario: 'I think they make up laws to suit the occasion.'

'*Muh!*' he said.

By the time he was eighteen he had turned his back on Sicily as any Sicilian who 'makes it' has to do. He cited Pirandello and Verga: 'People are surprised when you tell them these artists were Sicilian.'

'Any news?' we asked each other on yet another of these wintry afternoons at Il Gabbiano.

'This enforced stay will push me to write a book sooner or later. But no one can live in this place when they feel so alienated and disenchanted. These people believe they know me, but the truth is they have absolutely no idea! By the autumn I have to make my choice — but it isn't much of a choice, somehow I've got to get out of here.'

I looked at him and remembered something he had said to me last year when I was upset about having to leave.

'Remember, *cara* Jenny, life is beautiful because it is varied.' But his was stoicism akin to despair.

A scarlet sun glared down at the grey sea. It was cold tonight, I had to agree, and everyone on the bus appeared dressed for the Arctic. My apartment looked like a Turkish bath, so much humidity, the windows were all steamed up. I settled with my supper and a glass of red wine, feeling nostalgic for the past, for the life that other Jenny used to live. I thought of Art and the long letter he wrote, saying he would never forget the day we spent together. Neither would I: a chance meeting at a beach trattoria, a snorkelling expedition when the current swept me out to sea and this charming American rescued me. It was a day that went on and on and extended into evening.

It was mystical the way we met and the conversation and the beach, and you were lost and found again. And that marvellous place you took me to eat: Neptune's Grotto, wow! The linguine… love the name, and those candles. It was love and death and all those big things. I think of you often. Where are you? In your beloved Sicily still?

Sergio's rapping on the door broke in on this dream. His face was half-hidden by a huge scarf. He was just off to take his dog, Duke, for a walk. 'I've been trying to contact you all afternoon,' he said a trifle reproachfully. 'We've had a call from Messina, there's an appointment on Friday.'

I should have been pleased. Of course I was. But there was a part of me that had become used to this time of waiting without hope, almost Sicilian really with its sense of fatalism. I'd come to enjoy my complicit afternoons with Mario.

TWENTY-ONE

A Time
in Rome

*I*n *Paradise Lost* John Milton compares Satan to a will o'
the wisp tempting Eve to eat from the Tree of Knowledge.
To me that seemed to sum up my situation pretty well as I
pursued a goal that led me ever onwards but was difficult
or impossible to reach. Over the past three years I had had
tantalising glimpses of what might be achieved until Sicilian
bureaucracy crushed me into helplessness. There were times
when I honestly wished I could return to that naive vision
I'd once had of Sicily. Had Andrew not turned into those
backstreets of Castelmola, had we kept to our planned route
to Bar Turrisi for a glass of almond wine… if… if… At the
same time I knew it was too late; my eyes had been opened,
there was no going back.

On the morning Sergio of the NCDL and I arrived in
Messina for that long-awaited meeting, I remembered when

I had first heard its name. Years ago, during the brief time I spent with Amadeo, there was a charming, elderly man who occupied the apartment below ours. I gave him English lessons and during one of these he spoke of Messina.

'I grew up there and I love my city, but I would never go back to live. There is always the fear of another earthquake.'

He must have been just a child when the terrible 'quake of 1908 struck, destroying the city and killing so many of its inhabitants. But he was one of the lucky survivors. Messina holds no such horrors for me. I have always liked this place, with its view across the Straits to Calabria's San Giovanni. Perhaps because of its proximity to mainland Italy, the inhabitants seem to me more open and certainly they have their fair share of notable 'sons' – saints and artists, architects and composers. Only those who have experienced the destructive power of an earthquake have a different view of Messina.

On 28 December 1908, a huge tremor occurred, centred on the city. Reggio, on the Italian mainland, also suffered heavy damage. The ground shook for about 40 seconds and the destruction was felt within a 300-kilometre (186-mile) radius. Moments after the earthquake, a 12-metre (39-foot) tsunami struck nearby coasts, causing even more devastation; 91 per cent of structures in Messina were destroyed and some 70,000 residents were killed. For weeks rescuers searched through the rubble and whole families were still being pulled out alive, days later, but thousands remained buried there. Buildings in the area had not been constructed for earthquake resistance, having heavy roofs and vulnerable foundations. And as the inhabitants know only too well, it could happen again.

As we arrived at the State vets clinic to meet Dottore Donia, I was feeling optimistic. On the surface, at least, he seemed charming and eager to help. At lunch we outlined our hopes for a permanent clinic for feral animals in Taormina. Yes, he knew of a place and he would make some enquiries.

A few days later Sergio knocked on the door of my dank apartment, where I sat nursing my evening glass of red wine, watching television. He was beaming.

'Donia just called. He's coming to Taormina the day after tomorrow to show us a possible location for the clinic.'

On that sparkling February day, as we walked briskly along the Corso I truly believed I had got somewhere at last. Donia met us with a set of keys and we toured some spacious rooms in the now disused Taormina hospital. Perfect! There would be room for a surgery, a reception area, even a space where meetings could be held with invited foreign vets.

My journalist friend seized on the story with glee and once again an article appeared in *La Sicilia*.

During the following days, when I strolled in the Corso, people stopped to congratulate me on my endeavour.

Will o' the wisp! At one point I even received a contract and confirmed that yes, indeed, I would be responsible for setting up the clinic. But then there was a mysterious silence from Messina. By mid-February I was back in England, feeling defeated.

'No progress,' I told AISPA's Susan Dale. 'After all that time they kept us hanging around, nothing. I honestly don't know what to do next.'

'Why don't you go to Rome and see what they are doing at the Torre Argentina Cat Sanctuary?' she suggested. 'That began on a shoestring in the nineties but it's grown and grown. You might find some inspiration. By the way, they're holding a Gala Benefit evening in June and Dorothea will be there.'

A trip to the Eternal City in June! It sounded very tempting and, when the invitation arrived, Andrew and I decided to accept. Where would we stay? We wanted to spend ten days there and Rome can be an expensive place. Susan came to the rescue, putting me in touch with Deborah D'Alessandro, one of the principal people involved with the sanctuary.

'Hello, Jennifer,' came the cheery American voice over the telephone. 'We've heard so much about what you've been doing in Sicily. We're dying to meet you.'

The apartment she found for us was set in the heart of Rome's historical centre, with the Forum close by and the Colosseum a short walk away. We only had to cross a neighbouring square, dominated by the Papale Basilica of Santa Maria Maggiore, to reach a supermarket, where we stocked up on supplies. On our first evening we sat by the open window drinking wine and gazing out over the vibrant streets. The sound of Rome enjoying the evening *passeggiata* floated upwards. We couldn't believe our luck.

The following day, Deborah called and we arranged to meet her at Largo di Torre Argentina, a Roman square that hosts four Republican Roman temples and the remains of Pompey's Theatre. In 1503, the Papal Master of Ceremonies Johann Ludwig Burckhardt (who came from Strasbourg and was known as 'Argentinus') built a palace in nearby Via dei Sudano, to which the tower is annexed.

In the 1920s, Mussolini's town planners had ordered a

large department store to be built here. Old houses were pulled down and then, during the demolition works, the colossal head and arms of a marble statue was discovered, bringing to light the presence of a holy area. Work had to be halted and, as it turned out, this was very fortunate for feral cats.

Here, in the Area Sacra, live hundreds of them – big and small, ginger, tabby, tortoiseshell and black. Kittens play around fallen columns, cats doze on the temple steps or stroll around gracefully. Try to count them and there will always be more – a fluffy grey cat stretching from her sleep, a black feline under a pillar, having a good wash. These ruins, sunk below road level and with protective railings, are a safe haven for the cats.

I first discovered the Largo di Torre Argentina while I was on a working trip in Rome, around 1995. A friend had rented me an apartment at a ridiculously low price in nearby Campo de Fiore, which seemed to me very much the 'real' Rome. I'd shop for fruit and vegetables in the market that took place every day and in the evening sit at a pavement cafe with a glass of wine, people watching. I didn't know then but it seems this square once witnessed public executions. In February 1600, the philosopher Giordano Bruno was burnt alive for heresy, and all of his works placed on the Index of Forbidden Books by the Holy Office.

I was standing on the kerbside trying to cross a busy street when I saw a small white kitten launch itself out into the traffic. I was pretty sure where it had come from, the ruins of nearby Torre Argentina. Several times in the past week I'd stopped to gaze down on the cats who took refuge there. Circling the zone I found some metal stairs that led downwards in the corner closest to where Via Arenula leads to the Tiber. With the kitten in my arms I clambered down them and stood gazing around at the fallen columns of temples, the hollowed-out slabs of stone. There were cats everywhere.

'Can I help you?' A dark-haired young woman in dungarees stood there with a can of food and a tin opener in her hands.

'I've found this little kitten.'

The girl came closer. She wore rubber boots and I saw that the ground was uneven and muddy in parts. Carefully she took the kitten.

'She will be fine here.'

Paola was one of the volunteers and came here most days. She gave me a tour of this primitive cat sanctuary: a dim, smelly grotto with a rough concrete floor, minimal lighting and a tiny office space. The cat cages were a mixture of sizes and shapes, some new, some old, sitting up on plastic tables. Paola told me about the two extraordinary Roman women, Lia Duquel and Silvia Viviani, educated and multi-lingual *gattare*. They'd begun as so many of us do, by feeding stray cats, those who roam the Roman streets and populate its many historic sights. After a while, they managed to persuade the authorities to allow them to use the ancient site of Torre Argentina as a shelter.

'There's no running water or electricity,' Paola explained cheerfully. 'We have to carry buckets to and from the nearest Roman fountain. We've tried to solve the lighting problem with this big gas lantern on that table but the place is very damp and difficult to keep clean, however dedicated we are.'

Later, she wrote to me in England to tell me that my

little white kitten had died. Many of the cats had chronic colds caused by the dampness of the area and the unhygienic conditions spread the deadly disease of gastroenteritis. At least I had saved her from the Roman traffic.

All these years later I had returned to Rome, this time it was for the Gala Benefit evening, but also to meet Deborah D'Alessandro.

Dark-haired and vivacious, she was the image of Roman chic and I wasn't surprised to hear she had worked in the fashion industry until she was forty. It was then that things changed.

'I can't say I was really unhappy but my life was somehow in black and white. That was seventeen years ago. I turned my back on the States and took a house-sitting job in Milan. Gradually, I found my feet and worked in my field of marketing for seven years. Then I made another decision: I moved to Rome. I knew I wanted a change but had no real sense of direction. It was a hot, hot summer. I was walking by the Torre Argentina and someone invited me down to see the cats. I remember that a lot of them were sick and there was this small cave, where people were working. I met Lia and, after just a few moments, she said: "Do you live here? Why don't you become a volunteer?" I just froze. OK, I loved animals and I had always had cats of my own, but this was a totally new idea. I believe there are times in life when the light bulb goes on and you know where you are meant to be going.

'I worked with Lia, cleaning out cages and litter boxes, feeding and giving the cats their medication. There was nothing like the organisation we have today. At that time we

Above: A love of cats runs in the family. This is my father as a young man in the garden with Muffin and Crumpet.

Below: My own beloved cat Sheba.

Above left: *Gattara* supreme Elke with wonderful vet Oscar La Manna and Katarina, who brought them together.

Above right: Tireless cat rescuer Helen soothes a captured feline.

Below: (*left to right*) Me, Helen, Davide, Guy, Justine and Valeria at the end of a hectic day.

Above left: Ginger was extremely poorly, and her body covered in scabs, before she was treated.

Above right: A healthy Ginger, fully recovered from ringworm.

Below: Brighton vet Guy, who came to Sicily to help Catsnip, demonstrating a non-invasive surgical procedure to a group of veterinary students.

Above left: A very special cat lady Valeria hand rears a kitten.

Above right: A happy ending for Helen's tiny rescue kitten Gavroche.

Below left: Matriarch Macchia, who was rehomed in Taormina.

Below right: Beautiful Piccolino, who was found suffering from every parasite going, was nursed to good health and taken in by vet Oscar.

didn't have the shop, which is a great help in raising funds, just this small cave, and we desperately needed money. We knew we had one very important asset: this ancient site where Brutus murdered Julius Caesar.

'The area was always thronging with tourists. They would stop to gaze at the ruins and then you saw them do a double take as they realised there was a huge number of cats roaming among them. We encouraged them to come down and visit and then plucked up courage and began to ask for donations. It was incredible, the money we needed started to come in. Even today, we have no financial help from the local authorities: we survive on people's generosity. Now I work here full time and earn some pocket money to "feed my animal habit" by teaching on Tuesdays and Thursdays. My life took a dramatic turn the day I met Lia. It had certainly never occurred to me before to work in the field like this.'

Inspired by the arrival of one feline, Deborah wrote a book, *Nelson: The One-Eyed King*. 'A big white cat was brought to us, its eye dislodged, shot by a kid with a "toy" BB gun,' she explained. His imposing size and gentleness earned him a name derived from Lord Nelson, the famous English admiral. Soon, as he perched on the Roman wall, his furry mane fluffed over his large body, he attracted the locals. Tourists, too, paused to pay homage.

'People would come, calling out his name,' recalled Deborah, 'with gifts of gourmet cat foods.'

After a year or two he was the undisputed King Cat of the colony, often sitting at the first step of the stairs leading down, so the passing tourist could marvel and maybe even walk down to contribute to his and his fellow cats' welfare.

His fame grew. Meanwhile, Deborah's book, *Nelson il Re Senza un Occhio*, won a literary award in Italy and was translated into English.

Alas, Nelson is no more: his health suffered as a result of the damp conditions in the sanctuary but he is a legend and a symbol of the wonderful work at Torre Argentina.

It was time to visit the sanctuary once more, climbing down those metal stairs. What a difference from the last time I was here! The place was buzzing with activity. There was a well-lit central area, which housed the office and reception area for visitors. Someone was sitting at the computer, answering the emails that flood in every day.

'It's here we plan neutering campaigns while other volunteers talk to visitors,' Deborah told me.

A Dutch couple were asking how they could adopt a cat and other tourists were shopping for cat tea towels, cat calendars and, of course, Deborah's book.

To the left was a large, light enclosure, where cats roamed. Deborah introduced me to Tatiana, twice-injured before she found a safe haven there. Then there were cats who had lost their legs like the beautiful ginger tom who was nevertheless getting about quite well, as was the three-legged Don Camillo. The walls were lined with cages where other cats that were being nursed or had recently been neutered were housed. Deborah greeted one volunteer from Australia, another from the USA.

'It's a kind of United Nations here!' she laughed, adding: 'Our workdays begin at 8am with cleaning and disinfecting cages. Due to our confined quarters and the ease with which diseases spread, this job is one of the most important for our volunteers. Next, food is distributed to the cats in the underground shelter along with those that live permanently outdoors among the ruins. While feeding the outdoor cats, the volunteers must keep a vigilant eye out for sick or newly abandoned ones, who must be caught, treated, vaccinated, spayed and neutered.

'Some of the volunteers don't think they have the confidence to do this work so I do a convincing job and they soon get the hang of it.

'One woman visited with her husband and said she would be back to volunteer the following year, without him. We are also supporting 40 other colonies, which have a minimum of 20 cats and a maximum of 120. We liaise with the *gattare* and give them supplies of food, help them with medical treatment; in this way we are supporting 1,500 cats. We have certainly made a difference. At times when it seems impossible to go on, something happens that raises hope and encouragement. Perhaps one of our most handicapped cats is adopted or a generous donation helps pay another bill. In the end the hundreds of abandoned cats and kittens that have been placed in loving families and the thousands we manage to have sterilised every year make it all worthwhile.'

A day or two later we were all dressed up and making our way to the grand Piazza Venezia, where Italian fascist leader Mussolini once harangued the crowd from the balcony of Palazzo Venezia. We climbed to the top of a bank building to the wide roof terrace where the Gala evening was being held. After accepting a glass of wine, we gazed around. What an elegant Roman crowd! The men wore dark, beautifully cut suits; the women had not a hair out of place. But how that elegance swiftly vanished when the food was served. They fell on it as if they hadn't eaten for a week, pushing their way in to empty plate after plate. Talk about a rugby scrum! But British habits die hard: we held back politely with the result that we scarcely got a sandwich. Then came the raffle and here I caught sight of Dorothea drawing the tickets from a box. In contrast to many of the women, she was simply dressed but her smile outshone them all. There was time for a quick word before she was whisked away for photographs.

'Would you come back to Letojanni?' I asked her. 'I think Elke can get the *permesso* again.'

'Certainly I'd come, but not in summer again. It was far too hot.'

'I was planning on the autumn,' I said rashly, thinking, if she says 'yes' I shall have to get busy and raise some more funds.

'Glutton for punishment,' Andrew murmured, as we came out into the piazza again.

'Maybe, and I could do with some food right now!' I laughed.

We turned left past the illuminated Forum, which was swarming with tourists. It struck me that Rome is a place almost worn out by being looked at. People were everywhere; it was as if everyone was on holiday.

As we walked through this balmy night, I felt a surge of joy at just being alive and in Rome. I love this city and I always visit with a sense of coming home. We made our way in the direction of the Colosseum. Without saying a word we knew where we were heading: Luzzi.

With its long tables set out on the street covered with

check cloths, it's not a place to go for a cosy tête-à-tête. Conversation competes with all those who surround you. But we love it! Love the crazy waiters and the cheap and tasty menu. Luzzi doesn't serve some of the best food in Rome but it is fun, cheap and some of its dishes are pretty good, including the *Amatriciana*, or the *antipasto* that you serve yourself from the array of veggies and other goodies in the back, and you'll be charged depending on the size of your plate.

In the evening, though, your best bet at Luzzi is the pizza with a proper thin Roman crust and fresh ingredients.

As we ate, I thought of the saying 'Eat, drink and be merry for tomorrow we die', attributed to the Neapolitans, living in the shadow of Vesuvius. *Carpe Diem*, seize the day: this one had offered me such encouragement and the will to continue with Catsnip; it had been a particularly significant day.

TWENTY-TWO

I Have
My Doubts

The scene is surreal. I'm standing in the classroom of a Sicilian school talking to the children about cats. I can hardly hear myself speak. Under the beady eye of their teachers, they may be well behaved but my appearance is treated like something of an entertainment. Hands flutter, they all want to speak at once.

'*Signora*, I have two kittens I found in the street. One of them has something wrong with his eye. What should I do?'

'I love my dog, *Signora*, but my parents don't want him in the house.'

'*Signora*! *Signora*! Listen, I want to be a vet when I grow up. I want to help all the animals. What must I do?'

Lovely, innocent children who have yet to come under their parents' mistrust of animals, the general ignorance of these creatures as sentient beings. Over the course of that week I visited five schools. At one, where I had distributed fifty of my booklets on animal welfare, the children crowded round me.

'*Signora*, please will you sign it?'

'And mine, and *mine*!'

Talk about being a celebrity for five minutes.

These school visits were a welcome break from my second catch/neuter/return week in Letojanni, which I had found upsetting and difficult.

After my return from Rome to England, the summer of 2005 had been a busy one. Catsnip had taken over my life but it was time to concentrate on work. My play, *End of Story*, had been chosen as one of six to form a theatre trail during the Arundel Festival; now we went into rehearsal. The play dealt with the relationship between Harold Shipman and his wife, Primrose. I'd always been fascinated by the evil doctor and his apparent ease in murdering so many of his patients before he was found out. What intrigued me even more was the way Primrose supported him without question. What kind of woman can sit in court and suck sweets while her husband is on trial for mass murder? I had not only written the play but also cast myself in the part of Primrose and spent hours in charity shops, looking for suitable clothes. Primrose was not known for her sartorial elegance. As I am quite slim, I had to pad myself out to achieve her size. The play ends with news of Shipman's suicide and my unearthly shriek of horror echoed round the disused prison cells, where we were performing.

While all this was going on, I had to juggle fundraising and planning Catsnip's next trip.

'Education is an important part of this work,' Suzy Gale,

my friend and cat lady, had told me. 'Unless the local people understand the rationale for what we're doing and respect animals, it's a never-ending task.'

She was right and what better place to start than with young people?

'Dogs Trust do a lot of educational material,' Suzy added. 'I'll put you in touch with Clarissa Baldwin.'

Clarissa proved to be very helpful, sending me proofs of the publication the Trust was preparing for Romania. I planned a simple illustrated booklet and, having written it in English, persuaded an Italian friend to do the translation.

'I think it's a great idea,' Jayne at *Animals' Voice* enthused. 'We take wildlife into schools and talk to the children about their welfare. I'll pass it on to the others.'

A few days later she called and said the magazine would sponsor my booklet, so off I went to the printers.

Then Elke called me from Italy: 'There's another problem. I've been trying to get the *permesso* for Letojanni but there's a lot of talk about mobile surgeries like Dorothea's being illegal. Yes, I know they allowed it last year but…'

The capricious nature of 'Those in Charge' was getting to me. 'Even though the local state-paid vets don't carry out work they are supposed to do and get paid for?' I retorted.

Elke sighed. 'That's typical Sicily. But don't despair, I'll go on trying.'

I'd been to the printers to collect my bundles of booklets and was almost on the point of packing my case when at last Elke called.

'I've got it! I went to the town hall this morning and they gave it to me.'

I flew back to Sicily on 26 October. This gave Elke and me a few days before Dorothea arrived with her spaymobile. Time to contact the *gattare* and check on the local colonies of cats.

My arrival coincided with two important religious festivals: All Saints Day and All Souls Day, 1 and 2 November. These days are very significant for Catholic tradition but their roots can be found deep in a pagan past. The Romans dined by their ancestors' graves.

The invisible world of the departed souls is ever present in the Sicilian psyche. When I lived with the Galeano family, I would often encounter the little *Signora* carrying a bunch of flowers and hurrying towards the cemetery to visit her husband's grave.

During All Saints Day, the whole family will spend time in the cemeteries with their dead. Lamps glow among the graves; there are flowers, and families picnicking. Often the gravestones are elaborate and display photographs of the departed. Far from being a day of sadness, it is one of celebration and love.

And what better way to celebrate than with sweets? At one time the Day of the Dead rivalled that of Christmas in terms of present giving. Even today, children are told that, if they are good, the souls of their relatives will return with gifts and sweets. Shop windows are filled with displays of uncannily real-looking fruits. They are moulded from *martorana*, an almond-based dough that is much nicer than marzipan and exquisitely hand coloured. Legend tells us that this tradition began in Palermo at the convent of the Martorana. The nuns decided to play a joke on the Archbishop when he arrived for his Easter visit. They created dozens of the marzipan fruits and painted them to appear natural. Then they strung them from trees in the cloister garden. The Archbishop drew his hands to his head in amazement gazing at the trees' miraculous fruit-bearing season.

Another spooky confection is the very white, almond-based biscuits called 'Bones of the Dead'. They are long and flat with the occasional knob and a tray of them will be amusingly irregular in shape, resembling a pile of bones. Creepy? A little. Delicious? Absolutely! The *ossi dei morti*, as they are called, are made with the season's first almonds, which are harvested in September. These nuts are always delicious but there is nothing like the intense flavour of freshly harvested almonds. *Torrone*, the chewy white nougat sprinkled with almonds, is another autumnal treat.

Several elements combined to make this trip unlike the previous ones. When Elke told me the apartment overlooking Isola Bella was on a long-term let, I was disappointed. I had begun to think of it as 'my' apartment. Where would I stay? Then Genoveffa, my *gattara* friend, came up with the answer: 'Don't worry, Jenny. We have an apartment close to the Pensione Adele. I'll give you a special price because you are doing all this wonderful work for the cats.'

This time I had no exquisite view across the bay, but there were other advantages. I had only to open the door and I would step out into the centre of Taormina. At that time of year when the evenings were dark, it was comforting to find life going on around me. Across the road was a cafe, where I could meet cat people like Lisa.

Gaunt with a small pinched face, Lisa seemed to carry

the world's worries on her narrow shoulders. Life, she told me, was almost too much to bear. Years ago, on a holiday from Sweden, she met Salvatore. There had been the initial romantic courtship, the coming and going between the two countries. Dazzled by Sicily and the kind of attention she had never found at home, Lisa had finally turned her back on that life and come to live with him. This is a story that I have heard over and over again of Northern European women seduced by the light and colour of the Mediterranean. It takes a strong woman, however, to endure the Italian male's attachment to his mother.

I asked Silvia, an Italian friend, to give me her views of the Italian male. This is what she said.

Italian men: hopeless *Mamma's* boys who can never cut the apron's strings or dark, broody handsome heartthrobs? Female foreign visitors to the country seem to hold the opinion that indeed Italian men are charming, handsome, romantic hunks who call all ladies '*bella*' and '*bellissima*' and think nothing of hiring a gondola complete with opera singer to serenade you from a Venice canal. Italian women, on the contrary, are not so sure. Maybe because they know Italian men well as they are their partners, brothers, husbands... maybe because they feel a bit guilty. After all – alas – they are often their sons and they have contributed to creating that strangest of creatures: an Italian man.

Convinced to be by God's appointment the King of Creation, an Italian man still shuns domestic work either completely ('*e' roba da donne*') in the case of more mature gentlemen or putting in a token effort that doesn't remotely approach a 50/50 share of the work in the case of the younger generation, even if nowadays most women work out of the house too. For them every opportunity passed is an opportunity lost and even the more seasoned men think it is their absolute right, nay, *duty* to flirt with all women but especially those considerably younger than them... one of the reasons why Silvio Berlusconi was sadly so popular for so long.

They also seem to think that testosterone prevents them from being able to hold an iron, learn to programme a washing machine or sweep a floor; but if they cook, then they are certainly worth at least two Michelin stars, of course! They are outwardly romantic with pretty strangers but emotionally stunted with their spouses: we love or hate them but in any case we are lumbered with them – unless, like me, you marry a British man. Naturally!

Lisa and Salvatore each had their own side of the story. She thought him a bully, he believed her to be neurotic, but whatever the ups and downs in their lives, on one thing they were united: cats. They might glare at each other but could then be seen exchanging a smile at the sight of a feline. Passionately devoted to cats, they treated them as their own children.

'We have six at the moment apart from the ones we feed,' Lisa told me. 'Two of them you neutered when you were in Taormina, but the rest…'

'I'll bring a trap up to Taormina,' I offered. 'And if you can get the cats to us, we'll neuter them, too.'

She gave me a wry smile. 'If Salvatore doesn't murder me first…'

The Pensione Adele apartment was rather strange for it seemed to be a repository for furniture and crockery. A huge sideboard with glass-fronted doors held an array of plates. Once, looking into the equally huge wardrobe, I was surprised to find a large gap between its base and the wall and found myself gazing down onto the shop below. But the bed was comfortable and I slept soundly despite the noisy nearby *trattoria*.

News had spread round Letojanni and once again there was quite a crowd to witness the arrival of the spaymobile. This time Dorothea brought another vet, Rafaela, and two German volunteers. The forty traps were no longer a novelty as they had been glimpsed enough times around Letojanni the time before. Quite a queue developed as local people turned up and joined in the cat-trapping exercise. Dorothea and Rafaela operated almost without a pause from early morning until evening. By the time we went for a meal we were almost too tired to eat. The two German volunteers were also dedicated workers. As one of them told me, their holidays are spent on such expeditions. Over the next four-and-a-half days we neutered 140 cats and 3 dogs.

I knew that a huge problem in Sicily is the many pure-breed dogs, which are adopted as pets but later abandoned when the owners tire of the idea or want to go on holiday. The number of dogs thrown onto the motorway from a moving car during the summer months is appalling. Some of them are rescued and find a loving home; others are far less fortunate.

One afternoon my phone rang.

'Jenny? It's Cesare!' he shouted. 'Listen, I have a dog with me that is very sick. Will your vets have a look at him?'

Dorothea looked up from the operating table and nodded. 'Yes, tell him to bring it here.'

The dog, a Great Dane, was skeletal. This big, beautiful creature was reduced to a miserable wreck, every bone in its body protruding. It slathered at the mouth and was in a pitiable state. We stared at it, shocked. Dorothea left her work and came over to examine it.

'It looks as if it is suffering from leishmania,' she pronounced.

Leishmania is a dreadful disease, which can affect the skin, creating awful lesions or, more seriously, vital organs. It is caused by a bite from a sand fly already infected from sucking the blood of a diseased animal or even a human being. We realised that this dog had probably been abandoned by its owners and dumped in the countryside, where these sand flies are rife.

'I don't think there is anything we can do,' Dorothea concluded.

'It's young,' I said. 'Can't we find someone who will look after it and treat it? Don't put it to sleep.'

As far back as I can remember, I have found it difficult to accept the idea of death and indeed euthanasia. As my Brighton vet, Guy, told me, when you are dealing with it on an almost daily basis as vets are, their initial experience of raw emotion necessarily has to be replaced by a patina of compassion. They are still kindly and warm, but this is weathered by watching owners say goodbye to their pets. If it wasn't they would become emotionally exhausted, compassion fatigue would take its toll and they could end up in self-destructive behaviour. It's known that those vets who don't manage to find healthy ways of handling the euthanasia of companion animals often look for a specialty in a non-euthanasia field or go into another profession altogether.

As far as we know, animals are blessed without this dread of death. Guilt and regret are human emotions: that sense of lack, of having 'let the animal down' when treatment fails. Animals seem to live entirely in the present: they don't become angry or judgemental, theirs is a simple joy of being with us. When my cat Sheba jumps on my lap and kneads her paws, she is asking: 'Notice me now,' and revels in the satisfying attention she is being given. I have often wondered what her cheek-rubbing purrs mean.

'Cats do this to deposit facial pheromones on people or objects in their environment,' Dr Meghan Herron, professor of animal behaviour at Ohio State University, is quoted as saying. 'The head butting is actually something that we call bunting.'

People assume that it's a sign of affection or acceptance into the feline's domain but, according to Dr Herron, bunting is a little more complicated.

'Rather than territorial marking or "claiming" someone, as is commonly thought, cats do this to mark something as safe... leaving a signal of comfort and safety; so you could think of it as a sign that they are "trusting" that person or environment.'

When your cat comes face-to-face with you and bunts or rubs, enjoy it! It's the next best thing to a kiss on the cheek.

If only we humans could be so unaware of time passing, of this enjoyment of the moment without the knowledge that life will end.

That afternoon I turned away in tears and went out into the sunshine feeling helpless that I could not save that dog. It brought home the terrible cruelty of some people towards animals and underlined why we were there.

When I related the incident to Guy, later on, he agreed with Dorothea that it had been the only outcome.

'We have to learn to differentiate between companion animals whose owners are prepared to nurse and medicate them,' he explained. 'It's harsh, but true that unless a feral animal has a problem that can be treated with first aid they can't be helped with anything more serious. The criteria has to be quality of life and that may come down to putting them to sleep.'

Our only other casualty was a cat, which escaped and went under a car. Less serious but annoying, someone stole one of Dorothea's traps and one of my expensive crush cages.

I was finding these sessions very stressful. The incident with the dog preyed on my mind and I saw again and again that ghastly sight; I was also having difficulty dealing with the team. According to both Dorothea and the German couple, every animal, no matter how young, must be neutered. It upset me when I saw tiny kittens being given an anaesthetic. Surely they were not sufficiently formed to withstand it? When I was out on a cat-catching trip, I deliberately didn't bring in these little ones. One day I went into a rickety old building and found a mother cat with kittens. They were right next to a road, where cars passed all the time. The

German couple managed to catch them and I argued with them and so a coolness developed between us.

When the spaymobile and its team left once more for the ferry, although grateful to them for volunteering their time, I waved them off with a tinge of relief.

TWENTY-THREE

How Elke
Became a Cat Lady

*E*lke invited me to a lunch party at her house and it felt good to exchange my work clothes, jeans and T-shirt for a dress and jacket. It was 11 November and Taormina was enjoying a Saint Martin's summer. Autumn is no sad affair in Sicily; leaves linger on the trees and it is warm enough to swim. Against an azure sky veiled with wisps of cloud, the pale globes of lemons ripen for the second or third time. Saint Martin, the brave and the good who cared for the underdog and sought social justice, is a fitting name for this season. Summer has not spurned us, merely divided its bright cloak and is saving some for later.

Autumn is also the time of the *vendemmia*, the harvesting of the grapes for wine. Years ago, some friends invited me to join them.

We were up before the sun to drive to Francavilla, close to

the northern slopes of Etna. From there we left the car and rode on sure-footed mules along steep and rocky paths into the mountains. I remember the sun-dried skins of a group of women we came across; their hair bound up in scarves, full skirts spread about them. They were having breakfast, they said, would we like to join them? Sicilian hospitality demands you accept. The bread had been baked in an old open oven, the cheese was made from the milk of mountain sheep; heavenly flavours eaten in the open air, washed down with country wine. Nine on *vendemmia* morning and we were already tipsy. But then it was down to work. If I'd been led to believe I was invited as spectator, I was mistaken: an extra pair of hands was welcome.

You take a sharp knife and bend double over the vines to clip each bloomy bunch of grapes until your basket is heaped high, then carried away and emptied into a large canvas sack. My teacher was a girl called Antonia, who was about fifteen years old. She had left school to work in the country. Soon they would be picking the lemons again, she told me.

The grape gatherers sang as they worked, one then another taking up the tune of a traditional *vendemmia* song.

When the last sacks were carried away we made our way back to the farm. Here, in a stone outhouse heady with the scent of fruit, the men trod the grapes emptied from our baskets and sacks. With their trousers rolled up to the knee and legs stained purple with juice, they tramped solemnly round, hour after hour, ignoring the hordes of buzzing wasps. Meanwhile, the crimson liquid trickled into the vats to ferment and become the new wine of the year.

When I walked once again through Elke's garden I saw

long tables were set in the sunlight. With her sense of occasion, she had decorated the trees with coloured lanterns and set the tables with flowers and wine. I spotted Stellario, an old friend, chatting to Ross, who was on a visit from America. Another guest, Mariella, told me she was psychic and said I would write a book – 'When you decide where you are going to live, England or Sicily'. Conversation ranged over many topics but by tacit agreement Elke and I stayed away from the subject of felines.

The cats were there, of course, slinking round the tables, fascinated by the scents of so much food. I felt the sun warm on my face and, taking up my glass, savoured the robust Sicilian wine. For a while at least, I put the events of the past week out of my mind.

Later, while her guests strolled about the garden in twos and threes, Elke and I were alone.

'Have you heard from Dorothea?' she asked.

'Not yet but they can scarcely have got back to Naples.'

'It went well, she is so efficient.'

'Yes, but…' I hesitated, remembering the strains of that week, my loss of confidence and a growing doubt as to whether I was right in what I was doing. It all came pouring out: how anxious I had felt, the difficulty of going along with the mission, neuter at all costs, even the attitude of the two volunteers.

'I found it very difficult this time, Elke,' I told her. 'And I got very upset over the age of some of those kittens operated on. I'm not sure I'm cut out for this work – perhaps I'm not tough enough.'

A grey cat had strolled up and Elke bent down to stroke it.

'I understand what you say, it isn't easy what we do. We don't start out tough but we can learn,' she replied.

I remembered then what she had told me on another occasion. We had arranged to meet for lunch and were sitting on the terrace of La Marina, a little restaurant near the cable-car station. *Bruschetta* had been brought to us, that delicious appetiser of grilled bread topped with olive oil, basil and chopped tomatoes. It is believed the dish originated in ancient Rome when olive growers, bringing their olives to the local press, would toast slices of bread to sample their freshly pressed oil.

Elke described her latest project, working as an exporter of olive oil and other Italian products.

'You're very enterprising,' I noted.

'I have learned to be a survivor – I've worked since I was fifteen and, don't forget, we lived through the Second World War,' she told me.

'How did you come to be so involved with animals?' I asked her.

'When I was living in Italy, my mother called me from Germany and asked me if I would like to have a well-trained shepherd dog. I agreed and some weeks later I owned Ajax, a really fantastic, fun dog. He had had an excellent training and listened and obeyed many commands. He could even fake being dead and on command wake up again. From then on this dog was always with me and slept in front of my bed. He was thirteen when he died.

'From then on I always bought trained shepherd dogs in Germany and brought them to Sicily to Villa Pace, Messina and Isola Bella, Taormina. I had very nice doghouses built for them, but the big problem was the heat in summer, also there was no branded dog food available as we have today. The dogs suffered a lot. I would not do it again unless they could live in an air-conditioned home in hot weather. Some females had puppies and suddenly I had fourteen dogs, a cat, a gibbon monkey and a beautiful English Weimaraner. I had my hands full, you can imagine.

'When we sold the villa in Messina, the new owners asked me to leave the last three dogs as watchdogs there. I always sent money every month for their food. Later on, I heard that one dog had died, which made me suspicious. I went from Rome, where I now lived, to our ex-villa in Messina. Nobody was living there but I knew how to get into the big park. No dogs! Then I remembered the place where they would hide, when they did not feel well: a large underground space. I went and called them. After a while they came slowly out of their hiding place. When they recognised me they started to cry bitterly and I could not believe what I saw, two skeletons without hair and their skins crusted by ticks and fleas. I caressed them and took them into my old bathroom, washed them with anti-parasite liquid, dried them; I put them in my car and drove back to Rome, where they slowly recovered and became beautiful again. Nero lived to be fifteen and Sabbia until he was seventeen years old.

'But living in a flat with two big dogs was not easy, not for them nor for us. So I decided after they passed away to have cats in future, and we got our first black Persian from Germany; his name was Flory. During the flight to Rome that tiny little thing managed to sneak out of his basket and suddenly there came an announcement from the captain over the loudspeaker: "We have a little black cat in the cockpit. Would the owner please come here and pick it up?"

'Swiftly, my young daughter, Adriana, obeyed. Thank God the captain wasn't superstitious about black cats, as are some Italian passengers!

'When we rented the house in Taormina, I remarked to my daughter that I would like to have a garden full of cats. And that is exactly what happened. One day there were five hungry cats in front of my door. Of course I gave them food but, at that time, I had no idea that feral cats should be caught and sterilised. Suddenly I had fifteen cats, later on twenty and then about thirty. At that point I asked vets who were friends what I should do. We started to catch them with traps so that they could be neutered and it worked. Now, after many years, I still have about thirty cats but all "done" and looking fine. Of course sometimes I get the surprise of a pregnant new cat, which delivers her babies in my garden. Meanwhile, together with some friends, we are managing the whole neighbourhood and its feral cats. We feed about a hundred cats and check on their health. Lots of time and money are needed! But when I complain a bit, Adriana says: "Mummy, you once said you wanted many cats and God heard your wish and gave them to you."'

Elke's guests were calling to her. She signalled she would join them and then turned back to me with her lovely smile.

'Don't worry, Jenny, whatever any of us do for these animals, we do with love and their best interests at heart.'

TWENTY-FOUR

Dogs Need to Be Rescued Too

*E*very year, I added more news to my website of Catsnip's progress. As time went by, I received an increasing number of emails from animal lovers visiting Sicily, who had found Catsnip. Several of them were concerned about dogs, too. One of these was Christine:

> I was on a cruise, which stopped at the port of Trapani on the west coast of Sicily. We walked through the town and found a small square with shrines let into the walls, presumably to celebrate the fishing industry of the town. Here I saw a large dog lying in the shade without moving and I wondered if it was ill. The thing that struck me particularly was that its claws were excessively overgrown. I've been thinking about it ever since. Can you help?

I didn't know how to reply to this – my work so far had been on the eastern side of the island and I had no contacts in Trapani. However, a few days later, I had an email from Susie telling me of her visit with her friend Esther to Cefalù on the northern coast. Here, they had fallen in love with a little grey cat and had fed her. One evening she had brought one of her kittens to them. They wondered who would feed her when the hotel closed. Was it a very complicated process to adopt her and have her in their home? Always a ponderable question, it may seem a kindly act but, as with my experience in Letojanni, sometimes taking a cat away from her territory is not the best thing to do. When I realised what dedicated animal lovers they were, I told them about the Trapani dog and my sense of helplessness.

'Don't worry, we'll find it,' Susie replied. And they did. Their journey involved an heroic 400-kilometre (248-mile) round trip but, with Christine's map, they located the dog.

'He's a Dalmatian,' Susie reported. 'He wagged his tail when we spoke to him. He seems to be known in the area. We've called him Tito. I don't think he's ill, though the claws do need to be cut.'

What next? I'd begun to create a database of local animal welfare contacts. One of these was the international organisation for the protection of animals, OIPA. Its primary aims, I learned, are to raise awareness of the correct care of animals and defend their rights, including a campaign to help feral animals, oppose hunting and any form of ill treatment. The group also collaborates with people in the medico-veterinary sector to abolish vivisection and promote medical research devoid of the use of animals as laboratory guinea pigs. I contacted Raimonda, local delegate of OIPA for Trapani. When I spoke to her on the phone she told me she had gone several times to look for Tito. She, too, thought he was a neighbourhood dog. After a few weeks she wrote to me telling Tito's story, except that the dog was a female and her name was now Dina.

Dina was found on the motorway in 2003 with an exposed fracture to her back leg and was taken to the Trapani Dog Shelter. Several weeks passed before she was operated on. Because of this delay, at the time of the operation the bone was already set, provoking another fracture, and it was necessary to use a metal rod to align the leg. The operation didn't go very well because the bone was already fragile and for this reason it set badly. It was thought she would be liberated into the neighbouring territory, but then found preferable to put her in the shopping zone as a neighbourhood dog, considering her difficulty in walking and that here she would be loved, fed and cared for by all the residents. A young woman treated her with anti-flea and tick medicine and she explained to everyone the dog's state of health.

After a few months, when she was sleeping under one of the parked cars, she sustained another injury. Fortunately, this time there was only bleeding and bruising, nothing serious and she was treated with antibiotics and medication on the spot. About four years ago, she was put back in the dog shelter because some fishermen noticed she had sores as a result of her considerable body fat. Dina was generally not very mobile. Everyone was feeding her so there was always available food under her nose and she didn't need to make any effort. Taken to the vet, he found she had developed a heart problem and he said she must slim down. She passed the summer in the dog shelter, where she was treated and stabilised then taken back to her place, where she was welcomed with affection.

Dina lived with two other friends, one called Neve who is still there, and another, Little Dog Moon, who in 2010 was skewered through the throat by the spear of a gate in a shop door. Having witnessed the death of her playmate, Dina is now isolated and hardly comes through the gate. For ten years she has lived by the sea and, for a dog, ten years is almost an entire lifetime.

'Some people in Verona would like to donate a kennel for Dina and one for Neve. I have to speak to the town hall to ask authorisation and to position and fix them in place because someone might steal them. I hope to give you some positive news soon,' Raimonda concluded.

Paolina found me on Facebook and wrote to tell me about her work with dogs: 'I'd been working in Germany for a number of years and when I returned to Italy I was shocked by what I saw. I found myself confronting an extremely cruel reality – animals considered to be nothing, maltreated, poisoned, slaughtered and abused. This was the order of the day; also there were many starving dogs. In order to help them I have committed all my belongings, reducing myself to poverty, and obtained, as well, a marginalisation on the part of my countrymen. Because of this, my aim is to achieve a secure location where I can keep the dogs, make sure they have enough to eat, care for them and find good adoptive homes.'

Over the next few months she described the fight to achieve her dream. The family owned a piece of land but she needed to raise enough funds to satisfy the authorities it would be built according to their regulations. At the same time, she waged a daily battle against hostile neighbours and animal cruelty.

'I scarcely sleep,' she told me. 'At night I go to the outlying farms where there are starving dogs. And I am forever finding injured animals and female dogs, which have just given birth. Sometimes I feel so tired I don't know how I can go on.'

In spite of all these difficulties, Paolina has built her refuge, thanks to the generous donations I was able to send to her.

Animal rights is the last bastion of morality; there are still so many people who do not recognise these creatures are sentient beings, just like us. The only difference is that they cannot speak our language. And because they can't speak for themselves they undergo all kinds of cruelty and exploitation. We have to be grateful to those students of animal behaviour who are accepting that animals are feeling and thinking beings with complex emotional lives. They feel joy, love, pain, fear, anxiety, sorrow; they demonstrate humour too. The range of animal sentience that is now being recognised is astounding – rats who chuckle when being tickled and come back for more, turkeys who are so clever that they have been known to hold up heavy traffic in order to let their babies cross the road. Parrots are a whole amazing story in themselves: they have the emotional age of a toddler and the intelligence of a five-year-old child. They bond so deeply with either their parrot or human companions that parting and separation cause them great suffering, so much so that they have been known to stop eating and die as a result of this.

Mother Theresa of Dogs was a badly abused and neglected greyhound locked up and left to die. She was finally rescued and taken to an animal sanctuary, emaciated and shivering with fear. However, as time went by, she grew in confidence with the love and care she received and has ended up becoming the sanctuary's resident surrogate mother. She welcomes all the new arrivals, providing them with the love and care their bruised souls so badly need.

I have always loved animals, especially the cat, this divine creature: a pygmy lion who loves mice, hates dogs and patronises human beings. Latest statistics from the Pet Population Report show that there are 8 million of them in British households – 17 per cent of the population shares its family with a cat. Worshipped or reviled in the past, there is no doubt about it: felines reign over many of today's households.

They have even usurped the selfie and taken command of the Internet, where photos and videos are concerned, according to research conducted by network Three. There is also a trend towards Social Petworking – with over 350,000 cat owners creating social media accounts for their feline.

A fifth of those who created an account for their cat said they'd done so because they felt their pet was more interesting than themselves, and 15 per cent share content in the hope their animal will become a viral superstar.

I have certainly noticed the increase in sharing funny or cute pet pictures online. Recently, I became addicted to the cartoon feline Simon. Thinking about it, however, I wonder what the object of all this attention feels about it. While dogs are natural comedians, tongues lolling, they often seem to be inviting us to join in the joke; cats take themselves far more seriously. Theirs is a natural dignity and grace. If, for example, Sheba botches a leap from floor to counter top when I am opening her food, she seems to expect me to behave as if it hadn't happened. Call this my imagination, if you like, but no cat of my acquaintance enjoys being made to look ridiculous.

TWENTY-FIVE

A Yorkshireman
and Marsala Wine

When you consider that, since the seventeenth century, there has been a large British presence in Sicily, it is surprising that our love of animals hasn't appeared to rub off on the local people. Many families settled there, occupying themselves in several fields, such as the Sanderson's essence distillery in Messina and the production of Marsala wine in the town of that name. In his book *Princes Under the Volcano*, Raleigh Trevelyan traces the Marsala story from the time when Benjamin Ingham first left Yorkshire to travel across Sicily in a *lettiga*, a kind of sedan chair but far less comfortable. He was making for Marsala on the inhospitable west coast – marshy and barren, almost certainly rife with malarial mosquitoes too. One of his countrymen, John Woodhouse, had gone before him and set up a *baglio*, a kind of warehouse where he had occupied himself with developing the local fortified wine, Marsala. But it was Ingham who refined it to such a state of the art that Lord Nelson ordered gallons to be piped aboard HMS *Victory*. Rivalry was stern between Woodhouse and Ingham, who eventually became extremely rich, allegedly the greatest tycoon England has ever known. Ingham tamed the Sicilian Mafia, became a Sicilian baron and moved in the highest circles of Sicilian society, commanding considerable respect by loaning money to some of the nobility. He also learned to speak fluent Italian with a marked Sicilian accent, tinged with a touch of Yorkshire.

Ingham's delightful house in Palermo, Palazzo Ingham, became the city's Grand Hotel des Palmes in 1874. His hugely successful Marsala wine business was eventually nationalised by Mussolini in 1927 and is now owned by the Cinzano Company.

It wasn't long before Ingham also met an attractive local lady, the Duchess of Rosalia, nearly six years his senior, but whom he adored. The only problem was she possessed a string of sons who were gamblers. The astute Benjamin, aware of the laws of inheritance, refused to marry despite the constant naggings of the Duchess. As the business continued to grow, he decided more of his family should come out from England. He wrote to ask his sister to send a nephew. When the preferred one, William, died of a fever, his terse response was 'send another' and so it was the lugubrious Joseph Whitaker soon arrived.

Gradually, a dynasty was created with the wives of the three Whitakers vying as to who could have the most sumptuous palazzo in Palermo. Joseph's wife Tina swept the board, entertaining royalty and celebrities from all over the world. Her sisters-in-law made their mark in various ways, such as Effie, who walked about the city with a parrot on her shoulder and was a great tennis player; also Maud, who wore vaporous tea gowns.

It was Tina who ordered the arrangement of the splendid Villa Malfitana in Palermo, while her husband Pip preferred to bird watch on the nearby island of Motya or else disappear into town to visit one of his amours.

On a visit to Palermo I had the chance to visit the Villa Malfitana myself. It is almost as it was in the 1950s at the end of Tina's life. Music by Tosti lies open on the stands in the ballroom but the grand piano has not been tuned for a decade perhaps. The polar bear skin rugs are still on the floor. As you enter the house from the main portico, your eyes are drawn to two cloisonné elephants originally from the summer palace at Peking and purchased by Pip Whitaker at Christie's in 1887 for £162 a pair. Nearby, are two 2.4-metre (8-foot) bronze cranes, also Chinese, holding lamps in their beaks and standing on tortoises symbolising the four elements of earth, air, fire and water. It is cool and dim in that grand central corridor and absolutely quiet. The great Gobelin tapestries from the Palazzo Colonna are still the prize treasures of the house but only a palace such as Malfitana could house them. Novelist and poet Hamilton Aide's watercolours, his bequest to Tina, hang in the silent, rather sad and dusty billiard room. In the Louis Seize room, there are one or two fine examples of Trapani coral work and signed photographs of Queen Mary and Princess Marie, Prince Oskar and King Victor Emmanuel I.

My companion somewhat bitchily remarked that the pearls around the British queen's neck were not nearly as big as those of the Italian princess. She had obviously been here several times and was impatient to be gone; I only had a tantalising glimpse. I should love to have spent hours there soaking up the atmosphere, wandering round the garden, with its host of rare plants.

We paused to stare at the enormous *Ficus magnolioides*, a fig tree planted by Pip Whitaker. It has a span of 41 metres (135 feet) and is reputed to be able to shelter 3,000 people. Sadly, then it was time to leave.

TWENTY-SIX

The Englishwoman Who Won a Sicilian's Heart

*E*arlier in this book I mentioned Florence Trevelyan, the animal and garden lover who left her mark on Sicily. I couldn't help but think how much Taormina has changed since this, her description of it:

When the weather was good I spent the whole day at the Greek Theatre reading. I saw the dawn there and the sunset. The old part of the village is very picturesque with simple little fishermen's cottages and sheep in the middle of antique monuments, and old noble palaces amid orange and lemon trees in flower also almond trees which have a snowy white flower. Many times we've walked down to the sea or climbed to the top of Monte Venere, which is 800 metres above sea. From its summit there is a wonderful view in every direction you look you can see the entire east of Sicily until Syracuse. Etna dominates a sea that is even more shining and there are so many bougainvillea, cyclamens and anemones. It is beautiful like a fairy story.

Florence loved Isola Bella. She used to take her terrier and greyhound there to bathe and would climb to the top of the island to meditate. In 1890, she bought the place for 5,700 lire. She cultivated her husband's land, planting olives, cypress and exotic trees, and constructed the little pavilions where she would retire to paint even when it rained. She collected parrots, canaries, tortoises and many other birds. Florence was to suffer terribly when, having conceived at thirty-eight, her first and only son died within minutes of being born. It was a blow that changed her whole attitude to life. From then on she dedicated herself to her adored husband and to helping the poor in Taormina. She was also godmother to eighty-seven young women, to whom she gave presents on their wedding days.

The cause of her death reminded me of the extraordinary Italian fear of draughts. They go to great lengths to protect themselves from the *colpa d'aria*, literally translated as 'hit by air'. This can strike in the eye, ear, head or any part of their abdomen.

You will see a man or woman swaddled in scarves even though a spring day may be sunny and indeed quite warm. Children play in parks looking like little Michelin men in their padded coats. Until at least April, they must never go out without wearing a woollen vest, known as a *maglia della salute* (a 'shirt of health').

Florence died from pneumonia, which seems to have been caused by her inordinate love of fresh air and cold baths. She appears to have scoffed at any idea of being 'struck by air'. Barrels of seawater would be carried to the couple's mountaintop villa, the Villa di Mendecino. With the windows wide open and the wind whistling through the house, she would stand in her petticoats while this icy water was poured over her. Her request to be buried in the family tomb on Monte Venere was carried out to the letter. It must have been a most spectacular funeral. People from every walk of life threw flowers as the coffin progressed past them. They recalled her many acts of kindness, the lasting legacy she had left the town. A procession followed the cortège to the lonely spot in the mountains under Monte Venere where Florence had chosen to be laid to rest. Among the mourners was her gardener, carrying an oil lamp to be placed in her tomb, and for years after, until he was too old to make the ascent, he kept the lamp filled and burning.

TWENTY-SEVEN

For the Love of Cats

I had always said I would never have another cat, not after the loss of my beloved Fluffy. He was the most beautiful feline I had known and, as is often the way with cats, it was he who chose to come and live with me. That November it was dark and dismal and I had reluctantly gone to the supermarket, battling my way through driving rain. As I turned into my road, I heard the sound of plaintive meowing and finally traced where it was coming from. Sheltering under a parked car was a beautiful brown tabby with a ruff of fur and fluffy 'boots' and tail. His amber eyes gazed at me beseechingly. He made no attempt to struggle when I picked him up and carried him inside.

I opened a tin of pilchards and he wolfed them down. The next day he was still with me. It wasn't until several days later that I discovered he belonged to a woman who lived across the road. Instead of being annoyed with me for this catnapping, she asked me to come and talk to her. Fluffy, she told me, was about two years old. She'd had him from a kitten and he had been a family pet. Lately, he had spent a lot of his time hiding or sitting on a high shelf. Then he refused to come into the house. This stressed behaviour had begun ever since she acquired a dog.

'I've been leaving food out on the doorstep,' the woman said, 'but it's not a happy situation.'

By then I had fallen in love with Fluffy and I think he was quite partial to me too. The solution, we agreed, was that he moved over to my house.

It is no exaggeration to say that I worshipped that cat and grew very close to him. He was a little monkey about coming in at night and my voice could be heard, echoing through the night, as I called and called him. But once I'd coaxed him in, he slept on my bed close to me.

Over the four years I shared my life with him, he used up several of his nine lives. About a year later, as I sat tapping away on my computer, Fluffy rushed in and sat quite still on the back of a chair. Sensing something was wrong, I examined him and found he had an eye injury. I rushed him to the vet and for a while it was touch and go as to whether he would lose the sight. I don't know how it came about but suspect it was someone with an air rifle. It took a lot of care and treatment before the injury was healed.

It took a while longer for Andrew to fall under Fluffy's spell. Unlike me, he had not been brought up with many cats. But soon he was as captivated as me. In the summer, we used to sit in the garden under an umbrella and there the cat would come striding up the garden in his 'boots' and demand that one of the chairs be vacated for him. Of course, I jumped to attention. In winter, he loved to lie close by the coal fire. I can see him now, my little lion with his fine tawny coat.

'He's like your child,' a friend once said. And I couldn't have loved him anymore if he was.

The second alarm came when once again I was working and Fluffy came silently into the room. I happened to glance round and was horrified to see that he lay on the carpet bleeding profusely from his back leg. We raced him to the emergency vet, where stitches were put in his deep cut and plaster cast. I still remember the joy when I picked him up the following morning and brought him home. It was just before Christmas and I abandoned all plans in order to stay in with him. I brought a mattress into the sitting room and slept beside him for several nights, the risky bond of affection forged ever more strongly between us.

Four years after I found Fluffy under that car, I was on the point of leaving for a holiday in Greece when I realised there was something very wrong with him. The vet said he could feel an obstruction and at first thought it must be a fur ball. Medicine was prescribed but he seemed floppy and lethargic. My sister Susan said she would look after him but I was in tears as I arrived at Gatwick. On the beautiful island of Kefalonia, I walked on the beach with Andrew but my mind was constantly on my beloved cat. When, two days into the holiday, my sister phoned and told me Fluffy was probably suffering from cancer, I made up my mind to return to England. The holiday turned into a nightmare. After a day trying to contact the rep who was nowhere to be found, we decided to take matters into our own hands. I packed my case and we went to the airport where we tried to find a flight. I was reduced to tears but Andrew was determined. Finally, when all attempts to get to Gatwick had failed, he managed to buy the last ticket for a flight to the West Midlands and literally pushed me through check-in. From there it was a three-train journey back home, during which the wheels on my suitcase broke. I was able to spend Fluffy's last two weeks with him before he collapsed and, in spite of all attempts to save him, died. Unless one has experienced the loss of an animal, especially in such traumatic circumstances, it is difficult to understand its effect on me.

I finished up with a nervous collapse.

'No more cats,' I said, the day we buried him in the garden. 'I will never go through this again.'

Seven years later, in 2006, Sheba came into my life.

'I have three rescued cats in my shed,' Susan, my sister, told me. 'Why don't you come up and have a look at them?'

Their story was an awful one. A man in Worthing had, for unknown reasons, sheds of cats and dogs on his premises. Several of them were black. What was his reason we will never know, although there is evidence that people use black cats in demonic rites and Halloween was fast approaching. Susan and some friends had taken the cats away.

Sheba chose me without a doubt: she climbed on my lap, settled there and began to purr. As I gazed into her beautiful emerald-green eyes, I was hooked. I don't know what had happened to her in that time with the man. Her tail hung in a strange way and she constantly coughed and sneezed streams of mucus. She wouldn't come out of the bed I'd bought her and so we nicknamed her the 'Igloo Girl'.

'We might have to amputate her tail,' my vet concluded. 'And she will have to be on antibiotics for the rest of her life.'

So I took her away. I treated her with homeopathic remedies and watched her thrive. She stopped sneezing and started to go out in the garden. The tail improved, although, to this day, it still has a slightly odd curve. Love was the magic wand and animals respond to it so well, but there would be other hurdles to cross in the years to come.

Fluffy's personality was very different to Sheba's. He was a neutered tom so the search for a mate was not the reason why he liked to wander. At the end of my road is a railway station and once I found he had strayed as far as the little railway garden tended by neighbours. The back garden and those backing onto it are Sheba's territory. If she manages to get round to the front she usually panics and meows to be let in. Fluffy and Sheba were not related, but Toby and Richard, two of my sister's cats, were brothers. The contrast in nature couldn't have been more defined. Richard, a tabby, was afraid of his own shadow. He was never happier than when curled up on my sister's lap. Black Toby, with his aristocratic nose, was a very confident cat and a hunter. Yet they were born of the same mother and, presumably, had an identical kittenhood.

So what is the reason for this? Is it Nature or Nurture? As always, genetics are one of the driving forces. Their influence can be seen most clearly in pure breed cats. Generally speaking, Maine Coon cats are very laid back. They are not overly dependent on their human family either. Instead of pestering you for attention, they will remain close by for companionship. I always thought Fluffy, with his ruff and 'boots', had a touch of Maine Coon about him.

Typically, this relaxed breed develops slowly, until maturing around the ages of three or four. Ageing does not eliminate their playful, kitten-like temperament and reputation as 'gentle giants' of the feline world. There's no denying the popularity of the Maine Coon. Even those who know very little about cats know this breed by name.

Siamese cats are very different and have a certain similarity to dogs. While many people see cats as very stand-offish, the Siamese is very friendly and loves to be part of the family. You can even walk a Siamese on a lead, if you want.

In ancient times, the Siamese cats were often used as guard cats. Their very loud cries were more than enough to alert everyone in the household to intruders. And, friendly and affectionate as they are with family, your Siamese will be much more stand-offish with strangers.

From my experience of my own cats, I know that, even if their beginnings were far from ideal, they both responded to love and attention. I have seen a remarkable change in Sheba over the years. Her response to human beings, even those she has only met for the first time, is outgoing and affectionate. When, two years ago, she underwent extensive surgery for cancer in her ear, the staff were amazed by her first reaction on coming out of the anaesthetic: wanting to be stroked. She will do anything to get attention, rubbing her head against visitors' legs and, when that doesn't work, lying sprawled on her back. This is a far cry from the nervous cat who for weeks stayed in her 'igloo' when she first arrived. It has proved to me that cats, far from being aloof as so many people think, respond to us not only because we feed them.

TWENTY-EIGHT

Catsnip Arrives in the House of Commons

After all our telephone conversations, I was finally to meet animal welfare campaigner Suzy Gale and her husband, Roger. In December 2005, they invited me to the House of Commons for the launch of their new animal welfare project. As I walked along Victoria Street, with the sound of Big Ben chiming the hour, I wondered about the protocol for getting inside Westminster. I prowled round the building until I eventually found the side entrance. It was while my bags were being scrutinised by security that it suddenly struck me just how far I had come with Catsnip. As if in a series of snapshots, I saw Giulio and me prowling Castelmola in search of the injured cat and then the sad face of Antonella; I seemed to hear Elke's cry of triumph as yet another feral entered our traps. Frank, Genoveffa, Dorothea… all swam through my mind. What a journey I had made in their company! Now I was to meet representatives of some of the UK's leading animal charities and share with them the championing of those who could not speak for themselves.

A petite blonde woman was waiting to greet me in the central lobby, a lofty stone octagonal space with a tiled floor. 'So lovely to meet you at last,' said Suzy in a slightly husky voice.

Roger shook my hand, then led the way along what seemed a maze of corridors, where he was constantly greeted by colleagues – I felt like royalty.

The meeting was to present the idea of launching an organisation whose goal was to alleviate the situation of feral animals, particularly cats and dogs throughout Europe. What interested me was that it would be angled towards helping those working on a small scale, such as Catsnip.

Said Suzy: 'We don't intend to cut across the admirable work already carried out by various organisations in the field but rather to fill a gap in the market.'

'But surely there are organisations already dealing with this?' a voice cut in.

Suzy was quick to pursue this. 'Yes, of course there are, on the larger scale, but I think the idea of "one person can make a difference" might be embodied in other ways. For example, there is the tourist who sees a case of severe animal abuse or neglect and has no reference point or access to a website that could offer advice. I also think there is a need for support for small neutering and sanctuary projects, which at the moment is not catered for.'

As Suzy confirmed, she had several years of hands-on experience: 'Some years ago, Roger and I visited the

St Nicholas Monastery of the Cats at Akrotiri in Cyprus. What we saw had a profound effect on us both. There were hundreds of sick and dying cats and kittens, exposed to the scorching sun and multiplying unchecked. I launched the Cross Cats Project, and, together with Professor Ronald Jones of Liverpool Veterinary School, we took groups of veterinary graduates to Cyprus. Over a period of three years, hundreds of cats were caught, neutered and returned to their original territories. It was an invaluable experience of hands-on work in basic conditions for these young people.'

But, she added, when this project was forced to be discontinued, sadly the improvement did not last as the cats then went on to multiply again, with local vets refusing to continue the work.

'I was left with a small sum of money in the account. I approached a large international charity, which showed an interest in such work, but has not pursued it.'

Suzy then received a plea from 'a lone voice on the Internet' that one person can make a difference. She took up the cudgels and developed the idea of tourism and animal welfare. Since then she has been cheered by requests across the political parties seeking advice about animal welfare:'The Conservative Animal Welfare Group receives large numbers of requests for information, advice and assistance. Perhaps there is a need for such an independent organisation to be formed to deal with these matters?'

'I'd like to point out the number of stray dogs which are killed in the UK,' put in Clarissa Baldwin of Dogs Trust. 'Even though this number is reduced, we still have to clean up our act.'

She was more positive about the 'Romanian Experience', where dogs had been neutered and returned to their location with no great hope of many being adopted. In fact, in two years, they had achieved an amazing number of 800 adoptions.

Suzy caught my eye. It was my turn to stand up and describe the work of Catsnip. As I heard myself speak and saw the rapt expressions around me, all my doubts seemed to fade. I had been strong; acted when others just sighed and turned away. Elke had been right when she'd said 'someone has to care about them'. I'd felt so much alone but was now surrounded by people who had dedicated their lives to needy animals in a similar way. Amid a burst of applause I sat down.

'I've travelled all over the place since the Cyprus experience,' Suzy continued, 'and it's become clear that very little is being done to deal with the problems with feral and stray animals; many horses and donkeys are also neglected by their owners. The situation seems to be the norm in many tourist destinations.'

She smiled at me. 'I've also realised that many small projects, sanctuaries and other groups in the UK and overseas need support, both in terms of finance and advice.'

'Oh, yes!' I couldn't help murmuring. 'When I began, I knew nothing – I just had to pick it up as I went along.'

This new initiative, Suzy outlined, would include a website offering advice to others trying to set up similar projects to Catsnip, information on the purchase of equipment and data on available vets and volunteers willing to help.

'My view is that far too many tourist areas neglect the local stray animals; they are willing to take money from tourists but not to address the problems. We now expect to be in a position to bring pressure to bear and to assist those people working in the field, to alleviate these problems with a programme of catch/neuter/return and in the long term we would obviously like to see well-run shelters established. Animal lovers have the right to go on holiday and enjoy themselves, knowing that the local stray population are receiving the care and attention they would wish.'

And so Animals Worldwide was launched. A drink in the House of Commons bar, another new experience for me, and then I was walking back along Victoria Street to catch my train. What a day it had been!

TWENTY-NINE

Life at Villa Pace

*E*ver since I met Elke in 2003, I had become intrigued by her story. It was an amazing journey that had brought her from her young life in Germany during the aftermath of the Second World War to this woman who lived atop a rocky crag with its magnificent view of Isola Bella. Although she had told me she always loved animals, I marvelled at how she had come to be a *gattara*, caring for so many cats.

In my mind's eye I saw a young woman with a stunning smile welcoming passengers at the Lufthansa desk in Frankfurt. Had one of them been the Marchese Emilio Bosurgi? Was it then her grace and warm personality had won his heart?

It was a meeting that would transform her life, taking her from the world of aviation into the literally golden industry of the Sicilian orange.

Springtime in Sicily is fragrant with the *zagara*, the local name for orange blossom; the island is renowned for its citrus fruit, and Lentini in the province of Syracuse is an important area for their cultivation. One year I took a trip to Lentini and watched the oranges being sorted at incredible speed and packed carefully for export. The father of my friend, Davide, gave me a lesson in the many varieties and many a tasting. My favourite, the Moro, has deep-red flesh and even the rind has a blush. The flavour is stronger and the aroma more intense than a regular orange. Lately it has been praised for the high level of antioxidants it contains. With its hint of raspberry the Moro's flavour is less sweet than the Tarocco or the Sanguinello. The Moro variety is believed to have originated at the beginning of the twelfth century as a mutation of the Sanguinello Moscato. Peel a Moro and divide it into segments and you will see flesh that may range from orange veined with ruby to vivid crimson to almost black.

It must have seemed like a fairy tale when Elke moved with her husband into the sumptuous Villa Pace surrounded by its luxuriant gardens in Messina, where they spent the winters from 1960 to 1982. The villa has been described as a place of the soul. Its history is another example of the influence of the British on Sicily. It was 1817 when the English businessman William Sanderson transferred to Messina to set up his business specialising in citrus extracts. The society of that time was sharply divided between the materialist middle classes and the misery of the poor. Wealthy people like Sanderson lived on the Via Consolare Pompea. Villa Pace was one of the most important buildings in Messina and the lifestyle in the time of Sanderson must have been very grand. In 1850, William's son, Robert Sanderson, paid 500 ouze for a piece of land in the Pace territory. Three years later, the year of his marriage to Amalia Sarah Child, a pre-existing small villa was enlarged and restructured as a prestigious summer residence, the Villa Amalia. At the same time, rare plants and expensive trees were planted, which over time would add to the moneyed seclusion of the inhabitants. Later, this great park was further embellished by the building of the elegant little Villa Casteletto – designed for the younger members of this large and extended family.

Scarcely a year after the death of Robert Sanderson, the earthquake of 1908 caused dreadful devastation. Villa Amalia was partially but irremediably damaged, while the Casteletto was totally destroyed. This building, which only nine months before had hosted the Emperor of Germany, was a pile of rubble. The earthquake also destroyed the Palazzo Sanderson, symbolising the collapse of the economic and social position of the family after almost a century of life in Messina.

After the cataclysm, William R. Sanderson, Robert's son, announced he had decided to sell Villa Pace. In February 1915, the new owner, Emilio Enrico Vismara, closed the chapter of Sanderson and that privileged existence in a dwelling with its fabulous view across the straits of Messina. Vismara was born in Modena in July 1873 and moved to Sicily in 1904. Here, on the island he went from success to success, among them becoming director of the General Electrical Society in Sicily (SGES).

From 1910, several significant names feature among the great financiers of the Society. Sanderson and Sons,

Oates and Bosurgi formed a limited partnership with the aim of developing production of citric acid. Apart from proving himself an excellent businessman, Vismara turned his attention to helping local children who suffered from consumption and rickets. His fortunes changed in 1929 and he gave up management of SGES and left Sicily. This was when the Bosurgi family came on the scene as new owners of the Villa. Giuseppe Bosurgi was a wealthy pharmacist who had been instrumental in helping enlarge a local hospital. He attracted the attention of Benito Mussolini, who offered him a title in recognition of his social conscience. When Bosurgi died in 1935, his work was carried on by his wife, Adriana – Elke's future mother-in-law.

Marchese Bosurgi was once a very rich man. He and his brother, Leo, bought Isola Bella in 1954, a lucky event for the dilapidated island, for they were wealthy enough to be able to transform it. Together they created a fabulous series of rooms and apartments sculpted out of the rock. It is thanks to the brothers that the island possesses some unusual and often exotic plants, as well as the naturally occurring Mediterranean vegetation. You can see the giant *strelitzia* and the dragon tree side by side with indigenous species such as white kale, Ionian lemon and the curiously named 'bluebottle' of Taormina. There are many insects, and lizards including one native to the island. A very colourful little chap, the scarlet shade of its stomach appears to fade or deepen according to the season.

Some birds live here the whole year, some for a few months and yet others may come to rest for a couple of days during their migration. You can glimpse the herring gull and the kingfisher, while the peregrine falcon and the alpine swift actually live on the rocky walls. Shrubby vegetation shelters hundreds of birds, too, such as the colourful hoopoe and little owl.

It is thanks to the Bosurgi family that so much and varied wildlife may be seen. They always worked in harmony with the inherent nature of the island and tried to preserve and embellish its environment.

Celebrities, ship owners and entrepreneurs all accepted an invitation to visit Isola Bella. Hollywood's Elizabeth Taylor was just one guest whose little boat slipped quietly across the bay to anchor at the foot of the island. Passengers climbed the secret path as if entering a fairy tale, orchestrated by the Bosurgi. All responded to the peace and privacy that had taken years to create. Renzo Barbera, a local poet who writes so movingly about his beloved Taormina, was another guest who remembers the scale and generosity of their hospitality.

As Elke told me: 'From about 1960, we were constantly asked to show the island to all the important persons who came for holidays, conventions or happenings to Taormina. I was always being asked for a tour of the place and everybody was driven for a sightseeing tour in a motorboat to admire Taormina from the sea. After that, we offered them a strong drink before leaving and, on many occasions, they enjoyed a good lunch at the pool, which Emilio had built, in between the rocks. We never invited people to come at night – that would have been dangerous because the lighting was very poor and people could have been hurt.

'It was during those years that a very prestigious award was launched, the David di Donatello, which would be presented at the Greek Theatre in Taormina, during the Film Festival. It attracted film-makers, actors, directors, producers and script-writers. The town thronged with celebrities.

'We had everybody as our guests; as well as many famous Formula One race drivers, important international company owners and managers, I welcomed scientists and writers, and nobility from all over the world. It was an amazing time of my life!'

The years have passed and Emilio is now over ninety, still in thrall to Isola Bella, the subject of so many of his paintings. From the terrace of the house, Elke can gaze towards that magical dwelling on Isola Bella and remember the happy days spent there.

THIRTY

I Discover the 'Real' Sicily

*T*aormina is a hothouse bloom, aloof in both a physical and psychological sense from the rest of Sicily. At one time I believed its romantic beauty was the real thing, though the view of Isola Bella certainly comes straight from an Italian movie and is the favourite image of tourist offices. Now I recognise this small town as an island within an island, offering the phoney face of the Italy travellers dream of visiting. It is the Sicily you read about in books or see on television, a feast for all the senses, but, as I have learned, it is a dream that doesn't come true.

Apart from my tours of the island as a journalist when I had stayed in good hotels and visited tourist sites, I had seen little of the real Sicily nor experienced the waste and poverty that sully this island. All this was changed in 2007 when I organised a neutering trip to Mascali in the province of Catania.

I can't remember how I first contacted Valeria, but during the winter of 2006 she and I spoke often on Skype. In her husky voice she described her work with L'Arca, an animal refuge, in the town of Giarre. It was the familiar story of cats and dogs dumped, of innumerable puppies and kittens, and the lack of compassion among many of the local people.

'We try to get them neutered but we're just a group of volunteers using our own money to finance the refuge. Practically every day we arrive to find someone has left yet another box of kittens or puppies by the gate. It never ends,' she explained.

I told her about the past years' work in Taormina and Letojanni and related the number of cats we had been able to neuter within a week. This was carried out due to the generosity of donors to Catsnip.

There was a pause and, when she spoke, Valeria's tone was wistful: 'It sounds like my dream come true. If only something like that could happen here. Do you think you could arrange it, Jenny?'

In spite of all my misgivings of the year before, I heard my voice say that, if she could find a location for the operations, I would organise yet another neutering week. She leapt at the idea.

'There is a vet near here who is keen to work like this. He's quite young and he has lived in the States and is very open-minded. What do you think? Shall I ask him if your team could use his surgery?'

Andrew's voice swam into my head: 'You're a glutton for punishment.'

Before I had time to give it proper consideration, Valeria

came back to me. Yes, Dottore Trefiletti would welcome the idea: 'He'll put a room at your disposal and your vet can use his anaesthesia equipment. There's also a van you can use for transporting the cats and several of the refuge's volunteers have said they will help catch cats. Oh, Jenny, I can't wait!'

I came off the phone in a daze. Of course I couldn't go back on my word but I really hadn't thought it through. It would be the first time I organised a trip completely alone, without the help of Elke. Up until now, she had always been my important link in Sicily and I realised how much I missed her practical approach. I needed a plan. Obviously, my first step should be to find a vet willing to come out with me.

Sheba's health had improved and she was beginning to behave like a less institutionalised cat; however, she had an ongoing ear irritation and needed treatment. During a visit to Guy, my vet, I plucked up courage and blurted out: 'I don't know if you would be interested but I'm planning to take another veterinary team to Sicily…'

Guy's eyes sparkled. 'Sicily!'

I could tell he was imagining the deep-blue sea and tantalising promise of cinematic Taormina and so I felt I had to be truthful.

'I've never been to Mascali. As far as I know, it's a provincial town not far from Catania airport. We'd be using a local vet's surgery for the operations but again I don't know what the conditions would be like. However, it could be an interesting experience.'

Guy didn't hesitate. He reminded me of his background in his native South Africa. From a very young age, he had tended sick animals and, in spite of his parents' misgivings, his ambition had always been to be a vet. For several years, he had worked with large animals in the bush. He had learned to treat big cats, not the small ones I was speaking of.

Guy set out to travel the world. His planned six months' stay in the UK turned out to be a bit longer – nineteen years and counting – as he found Sussex a great place to live. As with so many of the people who had come to my rescue in Catsnip projects, Guy's involvement had arrived at just the right time. I remembered Elke's remark when I had carried ketamine from Britain to Sicily that an angel must be looking after me!

'I'd be very interested,' he assured me. 'Just give me enough warning so I can arrange leave.'

So I went back to Valeria. 'I think I have found just the right vet – but where would we stay? I don't have a large sum of money available and I also have to feed the team, not to mention get them there.'

'No problem, I'm sure I can find something. Let me see what I can do.'

She seemed to have the same ability to get things done as Elke. Only a few days later, I heard the now familiar, husky voice.

'I've been in touch with my friend Vittorina, who's a great animal lover. She owns a small hotel in Mascali, where Davide's surgery is, and is offering rooms for your team.'

Team! This threw me into a panic. Besides Guy, we would need a nurse and someone with expert experience as a cat catcher. For the next week, I racked my brains but could think of nobody. Then I began to muse on how my need to do something to help animals had come about long before the discovery of Lizzie. I cast my mind back to an event that, within a few weeks, changed many people's lives, shocking them into taking a stand against cruelty. Like me, they had probably always loved animals in a general sense but the 'Siege of Shoreham', as it came to be called, was a catalyst. Starting out as an animal welfare issue, it developed into that of multi concerns, the cruel basis of the whole dairy industry, a change of attitude towards the British bobby – and even a xenophobic reaction to the EU.

THIRTY-ONE

Valeria, a Very Special Cat Lady

The local paper had been full of it: shippers were planning to use Shoreham harbour for the export of live animals to the continent. The local community was outraged and word went round, urging people to join the protest. A few days into 1995 on a dank, dark night, 200 of us gathered near the entrance to the harbour swaddled in scarves, thick jackets and gloves. We stood in groups and shivered, waiting for what? At that point we had no idea. Then the cry went up: 'They're coming!'

All these years later, I can still remember the shock of what I saw… towering trucks bearing young calves, heading for the docks. Sad, bewildered eyes peered through the slatted side of the containers: baby animals torn from their mothers, bound for the veal crates and a short life of suffering. The reaction of the crowd was amazing. As if we'd done this kind of thing before, as one we surged forward onto the road, our collective aim to halt those trucks. That night we took the police by surprise. There were only fifty of them and they hadn't been prepared to find the road blocked by angry protesters. After a half-hour of this confrontation, the trucks were turned back. There would be no shipment that night.

On the following night, more people had joined us at the port. What was remarkable and later seized on by the newspapers was the diversity of these demonstrators and their solidarity: a young man with dreadlocks chatted to an elderly lady with blue-rinsed hair; a man with a dog dispensed old-fashioned winter mixture to the shivering crowd. All ages, all sizes, all drawn here by this atrocity. I spotted a reclusive character who lived on the corner of my street and whose sole preoccupation seemed to be tending his roses. He stood a little apart from everyone else but nevertheless joined in our taunting of the police. The common cause broke down barriers, uniting us in a growing hostility towards the law. They were to become as much outsiders to our community as the faceless hauliers brutalising animals… but not yet.

Sussex Police had merely doubled its number, which meant once again they couldn't stop us. By now the media had got hold of the story and managed to turn it into one of an anarchist riot with yobs attacking ill-equipped bobbies. As is so often the way, it was all taken out of context. A balaclava-clad activist who scrambled onto the cab of a truck full of calves was pictured smashing its windscreen with a brick. It was an isolated incident, I can't remember it happening again, but it was shown on television over and over again so that it appeared to be a multi-attack. We didn't care; what mattered to us was that these trucks of young animals were leaving our shores for the slaughterhouses and veal crates of Johnny Foreigner and we were incensed, we would do all we could to stop it. At least, for the moment, we had succeeded. When interviewed, television writer and animal lover Carla Lane said: 'These people have done more in a few days to bring this cruelty to public attention than people like me have done by peaceful discussion over years.'

It was a heady feeling. For several days our little band had stopped the live exports and the country was talking about us. The day-to-day routine of life changed, centred round tide tables and news of when the next shipment might be due. Many of us reorganised our day around this… sleeping at odd times, doing little housework, alert for the moment when the phone rang and a voice said, 'I'll pick you up in ten minutes.' Everything else seemed like a dream, but we hadn't won yet. Whatever the Sussex Police felt as individuals, and I heard several of them voicing their dislike of this trade, they were duty-bound to allow those shameful trucks through.

The next thing we knew was they had shipped in 1,500 officers from other forces and block-booked several Brighton hotels to accommodate them, to ensure the passage of the trucks. It was to cost £200,000 a night. With the arrival of the Met, scenes erupted you would never imagine happening in Middle England. For many people, and I have to include myself here, it curdled mistrust for our police, which has never gone away entirely. Imagine riot police punching elderly ladies, throwing children against walls; wading in, feet first, on families sitting in the road. An exaggerated and heavy-handed attack, it was to be repeated at Brightlingsea,

Essex, where, in the same year, another attempt at exports was going on. There, another reaction by the local community ensued. As the battles raged for hours, then days, then weeks and then months, it led to over 300 arrests and many people being injured. But in the end, People Power won.

During those long vigils I talked to a lot of people or sat among them in the little cafe where we went for a warming cup of tea. There was Justine, a veterinary nurse, and Helen, who had left her cleaning job to join in the siege. The experience of that demo changed so many lives.

I remembered Justine had used her holiday leave to go and work in an elephant sanctuary in Thailand. Helen's one-woman quest to release ill-treated animals had nearly landed her in jail. I contacted them and, to my delight, they both agreed to join us. My team was complete.

We were all in high spirits when we arrived at Catania airport. I don't know what I was expecting, but the mental picture I had associated with Valeria's husky voice did not approximate with the glamorous redhead waiting with husband, Antonio Cundari.

'Jenny!'

We hugged and kissed as if we had known each other for years.

The Oasi Park hotel at Mascali was just that: an oasis of calm set among palm trees. Vittorina was waiting to greet us, a large, lumbering dog at her side. Over the next few days, I came to know her as a big woman with a chain-smoking habit, outspoken when it came to the driving behaviour of Sicilians, and with a deep love of cats. My room was right at the top of the building, a kind of attic with a sloping roof, and I loved it. After a hectic day at the surgery, it came to be my little retreat.

That night, we all assembled for dinner at the Cundari's apartment in neighbouring Giarre. It was to be the first of many during that week when Valeria conjured up delicious meals in surprisingly little time. Davide Trefiletti was working late at his surgery but finally joined us and sparred with his fellow vet Guy over a glass of red wine. We ate, we drank; it was a riotous evening. I wondered how we were ever going to get up early the following morning to start our work, but somehow we did.

I soon discovered that Mascali was a very different place from Taormina. Situated in eastern Sicily, low in the shadow of Mount Etna, the town has suffered many times over the centuries from both earthquakes and volcanic eruptions.

In November 1928, there was a disastrous event, which led to lava largely destroying the town. This eruption of Etna was the most destructive since 1669, when the city of Catania was overwhelmed. In just over a day, Mascali was devastated but there had been an orderly evacuation of its inhabitants. Families, helped by the military, were able to remove furniture and fittings from their houses. Evacuees were relocated to nearby towns, staying with relatives, friends or in hired apartments. A completely new town was constructed. The style was that of an urban checkerboard layout influenced both by towns in Sicily dating from the sixteenth to the eighteenth centuries but also with many of the buildings reflecting the 'fascist architecture' of the time. It was completed by 1937 and housing conditions were very advanced in comparison with other towns in the region.

Many people seem unconcerned about living in towns and villages in the shadow of Etna. However, the 1928 event demonstrated that lava is able to reach the lower flanks of the volcano within a short period after the onset of an eruption.

Davide's surgery was situated in a small side street and buzzed with activity. It was the scene of much coming and going of owners with their pets. Obviously, he was a popular and well-loved vet in the area. Above his main surgery, he had allotted a large room where we could store our traps and house cats in recovery cages. I'd bought more of the stacking cages, which saved space. Lovely Catherine at Metalcote, the company I use for supplies, had cleverly packed my veterinary supplies inside them and they'd travelled to Mascali ahead of us, by road. I established a simple checking in and out system, entering each cat into an exercise book and ticking it off when it was returned to its colony. Further along the landing was a smaller room, where we set up a makeshift surgery.

While Guy was setting out his instruments and arranging the operating table, Helen was on tenterhooks, anxious to begin. Very thin and wiry, she reminded me of Angela and I recalled that the evening before she had eaten like a bird. But she proved to have enormous energy and skill in catching cats. We loaded the traps in Davide's rather erratic van and lurched off. At other times, I went out with Valeria when we drove through small towns I hadn't seen since the time I used to visit Giampilieri, near Messina.

That village was set far back from the road, almost in the manner of villages built to withstand the Saracens. We had to walk for quite a long time from the station pass under a railway arch and by the side of a dried-up riverbed. All kinds of junk had been thrown into it: oil-cans, clothes, furniture and even, I suspected, dead animals. The streets were mean and narrow, the houses gazed into each other's windows as their inhabitants watched and gossiped about their neighbours. In winter, they would stand open fires – the *conce* – on the steps outside the houses and, as I passed, I felt a waft of heat against my legs.

We roamed over a wide area, setting the traps in the grounds of apartment blocks and in a churchyard where scrawny cats roamed among the tombstones of weeping angels and what looked like small houses inhabited by the dead. Valeria had done her homework well and knew exactly where to direct us.

One day, she loaded up her car with tins of cat food and told me we were going to visit Maria, a local *gattara*. We stopped in a grey, litter-strewn street and Valeria turned to me.

'Wait in the car,' she advised. 'Maria is out of work and rather embarrassed about accepting help but she takes care of so many cats and I try to help her as much as I can.'

A few minutes later, she called me over to where Maria stood on her doorstep, arms hugging her skinny body, clothed in a threadbare cardigan and floral pinafore. Her face was haggard, but she gave me a brief smile.

'Jenny is here to help with our work,' Valeria explained. 'Over this week we are going to catch as many cats as we can and neuter them. We'll be treating them too, so if you have any sick cats…?'

I met Maria's eye and wondered how she saw me. Our worlds were very different – a wealthy benefactor from

Northern Europe, perhaps? I was hardly that, but it was my turn to feel embarrassed.

Valeria spoke rapidly in the local dialect and Maria led the way to the back of the building, where there was a large stretch of waste ground littered with rubbish, old bicycles, oil drums… all kinds of things. Cats gazed at us inquisitively, then ran away. It seemed to me such a scene of desolation and lost hope, a kind of acceptance of fate. We fetched the traps and set them about the place.

Maria's dull eyes showed the first bit of interest. Again, Valeria spoke to her in dialect, explaining what we were doing.

'And it doesn't cost anything?' For the first time, Maria seemed to approve of me.

On another day, two young women joined us on our cat-catching expeditions. They were each called Giovanna, one a tall, voluptuous woman and the other slender and petite, prone to bursting into tears if she saw a sick cat or kitten. They were a wonderful help and got the hang of the traps in no time at all. Soon they took off on their own, triumphant each time they caught a feline.

'Big Giovanna', as we called her, was afraid of no one. Once a woman shot up her window and bawled across the road: 'You are murderers! You are catching those cats to kill them, aren't you?'

Big Giovanna planted herself fair and square on the pavement, hands on her large hips, and hurled back a stream of swear words, only some of which I understood. She was obviously too powerful an adversary; the window slammed shut.

On another occasion, the traps were attracting far too much attention. A small crowd had gathered, wondering at these strange contraptions and wanting to know how they worked. The cats were wisely keeping out of the way. Big Giovanna lost her patience. She pushed her way forward and stood like a policeman at the scene of a road accident, ordering the onlookers away. I half-expected her to shout: 'Nothing to see, nothing to see!' Not surprisingly, the crowd moved off sheepishly.

Davide was very interested in Guy's surgical procedure, the keyhole method I had already watched when Frank Caporale, the American vet, came to Taormina. One day, clambering up the stairs with yet another cat in a carrier, I was intrigued to hear the buzz of voices and a burst of laughter coming from the surgery. There was Guy surrounded by a group of young men and women. He was demonstrating this far less invasive method to them, gesturing in an animated way to make up for his lack of Italian.

'They're veterinary students from Messina,' Davide explained. 'They're still being taught the old methods – I thought this was a great opportunity for them.'

He was right. They stood there watching wide-eyed, as if Guy were a magician pulling a rabbit out of a hat.

The meals chez Cundari continued to be sumptuous throughout the week. I wondered at how Valeria managed to juggle teaching in the mornings, doing her stint at the refuge and helping with the cat catching in the afternoons before she took her place at the oven, producing delicious food. Some of the dishes conjured up memories of those I'd learned to prepare during the time I lived in Taormina. *Spaghetti Aglio,*

Olio e Peperoncino has ingredients that are deceptively simple but, when well prepared, it is very tasty. Garlic and hot peppers or pepper flakes are sautéed in olive oil until the garlic is pale gold. This sauce is stirred into al dente spaghetti; parsley is added and the dish is served immediately.

Fresh anchovies sautéed with garlic, and hot peppers in olive oil, deglazed with white wine, then tossed with spaghetti, diced cherry tomatoes and lots of chopped parsley, and topped with toasted bread crumbs was another of her almost ready meals – the *Spaghetti alla Siracusana*. There was more than a glass of Mascali's most popular wine, Nerello, to wash down these delights. Sicilian cuisine makes good use of the island's wonderfully fresh vegetables, which made it easier to cater for Helen, who was vegan.

As if she didn't have enough to do with all these hungry guests, during that time Valeria had also brought home several litters of motherless kittens, which Big and Little Giovanna had found, and she was hand-rearing them with kitten milk and a pipette. A truly admirable *gattara*!

I snatched an hour or so to wander round Mascali. The cathedral church is dedicated to the town's patron saint, San Leonardo, and was consecrated in 1935. It has three naves and preserves a marble statue dating from the eighteenth century, depicting the saint. The town, and its surrounding area, is littered with many ruined churches, the scars of successive earthquakes and lava flows. As I stood in the little square reading my guidebook, I could feel curious stares. One elderly man approached me and asked what I was doing there. Unlike Taormina, where almost every second person is a tourist, I felt very much the foreigner in Mascali.

Helen had no time for any such sightseeing. She appeared constantly poised to dart off on another cat-catching operation, impatient when we dared to stop for the sandwich lunch brought over by Valeria's husband, Antonio. When, in her view, we were not working hard enough, she borrowed Davide's van and went off alone on a reconnoitre of Taormina.

'Let's go back there this afternoon,' she urged me. 'I've seen at least two cats we simply must rescue.'

'OK,' I said, a little reluctantly.

It is not actually far away from Mascali, although those upward-winding roads taxed the temperamental van. What worried me was that the *permesso* Valeria had obtained for her area did not extend to Taormina. We would have to be very careful not to risk a *denuncia*.

We took the road that curves upwards, out of Taormina towards Castelmola, and stopped in Via Von Gloeden. Helen led the way towards a row of bins overflowing with garbage. She set down a dish with a little tuna on it and called softly. After a while, a small tortoiseshell cat appeared. She was scrawny and walked slowly; it was obvious she was quite old.

'Someone told me her name is Macchia. What does that mean in English?'

'It's pretty obvious!' I laughed. 'Look at the big smudge of black over half her face. In fact, she's a patchwork of them. And think about the milky coffee they serve here, it's called *Latte Macchiato*, milk with a smidgeon of coffee – it's a good name.'

Helen lifted the cat, which didn't protest. *Maybe she had*

once been someone's pet, I mused. She held her in her arms and stroked her: 'Well, Smudge, you're coming with us.'

The second cat Helen had seen in the same area was in a bad state. His fur was dull and matted, his nostrils caked with mucus and his breathing was noisy. Although obviously a large male, he looked wasted and on the point of death.

'The person who I spoke to told me that, although the local people try to feed him, he can't eat with this awful cold. I've called him "Big Boy", by the way.'

Big Boy might have been ill but he had no intention of going anywhere near the trap we set down. After a fruitless half-hour, Helen grew impatient. She went back to the car and returned with a large net. I had read about these nets, that they were used for animal catching, but had never seen them in action before. Helen was triumphant. After only two failed attempts, she managed to net the cat and gently carry it to a cage. He didn't put up much of a struggle – he must have been very weak.

'Shall we have a scout round, now we're here?' Helen suggested. 'I've a couple of traps in the van.'

'I think we'd better go straight back to Mascali,' I said. 'We don't want to stress these two anymore.'

As Guy was busy operating, Davide took in the cats and examined them. Macchia, he pronounced as being in not too bad health, just old and in need of feeding up. But Big Boy was another matter and required antibiotics and hydration. Thank heaven, he finally rallied but I think we had captured him just in time. When they were settled in two comfy holding cages, I glanced round for Helen but she had already disappeared, off on another cat-catching expedition.

Some days, I helped Valeria with her supermarket shopping, to restock for all the meals we ate. In this way, I got to know something about Giarre.

Its one-time claim to fame was as a collection point for the wine produced on the hills above, which was rolled down its main street in barrels to the port below. Today, its peculiarity is far more suspect. Little Giarre has come to be seen as the epicentre of the phenomenon of waste – a kind of architectural white elephant capital.

'That hospital took thirty years to build and it was out of date before it was even ready to open,' Valeria grimly observed.

Nearby was a partially built graffiti-covered theatre, where work had started and halted at least twelve times.

'We're not a big city, there are only 27,000 inhabitants, but in Giarre there is the largest number of incomplete public projects in Sicily. This waste is so amazing that some people have suggested promoting it as a tourist attraction!'

I wasn't sure whether she was joking, or not.

Later, I researched the most notorious of Giarre's eyesores. Here, you will find twenty-five incomplete structures built between the mid-1950s and the 2000s, many of considerable size, such as a vast Athletics and Polo Stadium, an unfinished near-Olympic-size Regional Swimming Pool, and a tumbling concrete palace known as the Multifunctional Hall. They are nothing but concrete shells, inexorably encroached by wild grass and cacti. Nevertheless, they remain a blot on the landscape.

Such buildings are a bleak reminder of the local politicians' habit of making impressive but ill-advised claims about what public works they could see to completion in order to secure funds from the regional government. Starting large-scale construction work has been a vote-winner and a way of creating jobs. It was also claimed to combat the recruiting power of the Mafia.

The week in Mascali had proved to be the most exhausting of all my trap/neuter/return trips. Looking back, I saw how the extent of what we had done, the areas we had covered and the stress of dealing with many of the cats, which were ill, had taken its toll. Our meals with the Cundaris had been the only time we could relax before another early and unrelenting day. As far as I was concerned, it wasn't only that. I'd had another attack of doubt about whether it was right to interfere with the feral cat's existence.

'That's nonsense!' Helen replied firmly when I voiced this. How I wished I could have her single-mindedness. My problem, I decided, was that I was identifying too much with the cats and their fear of being captured. I still hadn't learned the lesson of distancing myself, which is essential if you do this work. While I knew that, logically, Helen was right, it conflicted with my emotions. I recognised I was becoming over-sensitised.

The following Sunday morning, I came down to breakfast and felt as if I hadn't enough strength to lift a cup. I went to sit in the garden under the palms and lay in a deck chair, feeling I couldn't move my arms or legs. Utterly exhausted, I had the sensation of my muscles having turned to water. The others were flying back to England that day but I had planned to stay on a little longer. Now I was frightened of being left alone. Later, I was to discover I was suffering from volunteer fatigue, a very real thing and something experienced by many well-intentioned volunteers. Time to exchange burnout for balance. Vittorina came to my rescue. She told me to stay exactly where I was and, at lunchtime, prepared a light and delicious rice dish. That day she fussed over me like a mother hen. By the afternoon, I had begun to feel a little better and by evening, when Davide arrived, I told him I'd be fine for a little excursion to Taormina the next day: we were going to take Macchia to her new home.

It couldn't have been a better outcome for this elderly but feisty cat. Inga was a middle-aged artist who had lived in Taormina for many years and was a lover of cats. Her somewhat ramshackle house would never have featured in a beautiful home magazine but it was a haven for these felines. Old sofas were covered with colourful throws, where ginger and black, white and tortoiseshell cats slept undisturbed. Beyond was the wild garden where they could roam.

Macchia soon saw off a few of the younger cats with a growl and a smack of a paw. She settled herself on a wall where she could oversee the territory. I could tell she would become a matriarch in the safe haven we had found for her.

Helen would be very happy.

THIRTY-TWO

Etna –
A Brooding Presence

There was always a sense of anti-climax about the end of these catch/neuter/return weeks. After the hectic rushing about, the anxiety and general adrenaline buzz, you realised just how much everyone had contributed, even if, at times, tempers were frayed. It seemed strange to sit down to a solitary meal, that evening before I packed my case. Vittorina had invited me to stay for a few quiet days at her apartment in the area of Taormina that gazes towards Etna.

That ever-active volcano is a brooding presence in the lives of many Sicilians. The sight of its glowing summit against the night sky is awe-inspiring. No wonder *Mongibello*, as the locals affectionately call Etna, has been the subject of many myths. The ancient Greeks believed the mountain housed the workshop of Vulcan, the god of fire and metalwork. Far below, in the depths of the earth, he forged metals in his fiery cave and from time to time expelled the hot, molten liquid into the atmosphere.

Another myth spoke of a 100-dragon-headed monster, son of the earth goddess, Gaia, who rebelled and was trapped by Zeus for thousands of years under Mount Etna. Every now and again, he lost his temper and spewed out impressive flames.

Geological evidence has shown that Etna has been active for more than 2.5 million years. There have been 140 recorded eruptions throughout history, which wins Etna the prize for being the most active volcano in Europe. Like the Hindu god Shiva, the mountain has not only destructive but transforming powers too.

The lava that has engulfed cities and towns and driven people from their homes also produces a rich soil, nurturing a verdant landscape. An excursion to Etna, to experience the amazing views of the island from 3,353 metres (11,000 feet), is probably the first trip on any tourist's itinerary.

The landscape and the climate change dramatically during the ascent. At first, it is a terrain of fruit trees; in springtime the air is filled with the sensuous fragrance of orange and lemon blossom. Temperatures drop as you go higher. Etna's vineyards, where the popular *vino d'Etna* is produced, are vibrant in autumn as the leaves change colour. The area is punctuated by apple orchards, the hazelnut and pistachio, and here you will find the pretty houses of those who live on the slopes of Etna and have learned to understand the 'wicked witch', as D.H. Lawrence once described the volcano.

The climb continues into yet another landscape dominated by pine and chestnut trees, until you arrive in what seems to be the surface of the moon, of dormant vents, cooled lava and layers of volcanic ash.

Wrapped up warmly – at the summit of the volcano it becomes chilly on even the hottest summer's day – you gaze in wonderment at the stunning view spread out before you: a patchwork of villages and beaches far below, as far as Calabria on the toe of Italy.

One of the nicest ways to visit Etna is by taking the Circumetnea, a railway line that covers a 110-kilometre (68-mile) route round the volcano. The railway is an historic line, which has functioned since 1898 and was once used by farmers to reach the fields. Today, that request stop is still available on board. The usual route is to leave from Catania Borgo station and end up at Riposto. The year Andrew and I took the Circumetnea, we decided to do it in reverse. It was a Sunday morning and we were dismayed to discover there were engineering works in progress. A bus journey was involved and added yet more time to the usual three-hour ten-minute journey. However, it was certainly worth it. We felt as if we had stepped back in time, trundling along the one-rail line, as we gazed out on the majestic volcano and admired the lovely surrounding landscape, the typical olive and fig trees.

But it appeared we had been fortunate in managing to get the railway schedules to work. More recently, when we thought we'd like to do the trip again, we were confounded by the eccentric timetable and finally gave it up. We had planned to get on and off at the various stations and do a bit of walking but the leaflet I had picked up from the tourist office contained photographs but no information.

It seemed yet another example of Sicily shooting itself in the foot.

THIRTY-THREE

A House in Sicily

*E*tna rising on the horizon, often snow-capped, always
majestic, was the constant view of Daphne Phelps for
over fifty years. The English woman who inherited a Sicilian
house, Casa Cuseni, was another animal lover. I used to visit
her quite often and now remembered the last time I had seen
Daphne.

I telephoned her. The voice was sharp, belying her great
age. 'What's your name? Do I know you? I don't remember
you. But yes, come… come when you like. I'm always here.
Come today, tomorrow.'

It was a still, hot afternoon; the sun blazing from a perfectly
blue sky. Climbing up the Salita Leonardo da Vinci, I felt the
sweat begin to trickle between my shoulder blades, my hair
sticking to my forehead. The house was guarded by high,
blue-painted gates straight from a fairy tale, but there was a
confident air about it all – they were not locked. I pushed
them open and stepped inside. There were several flights of
steps that led past an old Roman cistern towards enchanted

and enchanting Casa Cuseni. I paused to gaze at it, climbed the last few steps to the terrace and Zitto the dog ambled towards me, barking. He was very old now, his black coat and muzzle streaked with grey. Zitto laughed at me as dogs do, with his tongue lolling, barking and wagging his tail at the same time. No sign of life; the house seemed to be asleep. Zitto decided I was not a threat and lay down with a sigh. I circled the building, wondering how I was going to make myself heard. Then I saw, at the side of the house, a small lodge and the next moment Concetta, Daphne's faithful housekeeper, came to the door and called across to me.

'The *Signora* is in, but maybe sleeping. Try again,' she advised. 'If you still can't rouse her, I'll telephone.'

So I returned to the terrace and stood for a moment to gaze at the golden stone of the villa, out at that splendid view towards Etna. I remembered the first time I was there when some American lodgers invited me for an aperitif before a party. It was an odd experience: separately and in different ways, they each fell in love with me.

There was movement behind me and a very old lady dressed in what looked like a nightdress with a cardigan buttoned over it poked her head out of the French doors.

'Good afternoon,' she said in a brisk, no-nonsense voice.

This was Daphne Phelps, grande dame of Taormina for over fifty years, who nevertheless remained the epitome of Middle England. She didn't remember me but she admired my 'frock'. I'd sacrificed half a day on the beach to make myself respectable – you did so when you visited Miss Phelps. Zitto was like a shadow at her side.

'What shall we drink?' she asked. 'Wine?'

I followed her through the shadowy dining room with its beautiful Arts and Crafts frescoes of figures in blue; there were garlands of fruit and flowers. In the vast kitchen she took up a bottle and corkscrew and in the meantime Zitto had cocked his leg against the table. Of course this had to be wiped up before we went outside again to sit at a table on the terrace.

We talked about her book, *A House in Sicily*, and its unexpected success.

'I've not been well-off all my life and now here I am, at ninety, with money. What do I do with it?' said Daphne.

I gazed again at the view, the tumble of terracotta roofs, the azure Ionian Sea; slopes of Etna, a sleeping giant. Purple bougainvillea spilt from a giant terracotta vase. I felt the glorious summer sun.

'More of the same?' I suggested.

Daphne Phelps' love story with Casa Cuseni began in 1947 when a cable arrived at the clinic where she worked as a child psychologist, announcing her uncle had died and she was to inherit the house.

'I warn you, Daphne,' said a colleague. 'People who settle in these out-of-the-way places become very eccentric.'

'My Italian was almost non-existent,' she wrote in her book, 'I had never dealt with property or had experience coping with Sicilians. I wanted to sell the house and return to England.'

On arrival, she was dazzled by Sicilian sun and colour.

'Nowadays it's difficult for people who've always been free to travel to realise the sense of liberation I felt after years boxed up in England with: is your journey really necessary?' she explained.

Soon she fell under the spell of this beautiful house and the near-perfect climate, like her uncle before her. 'Don

Roberto', as he was called by the locals, chose this location to create his vision. He left the original olive and almond trees, planting orange, lemon and grapefruit with flowering shrubs and creepers. Making use of the local craftsmen's skills and local materials, he erected massive outside walls, over half a metre thick. The spectacular view of Etna was seen between columns carved out of golden stone from Syracuse.

Daphne, taken by the warmth of the people and Taormina's beauty, was persuaded to stay.

'I had always been a maverick, enjoying the unexpected. I knew Sicily was sure to provide that,' she wrote. 'I would have its history, archaeology, folklore and botany and, above all, the superb climate and this magical house.'

She soon discovered there were certain principles that would guide her through this 'uncharted adventure'. The first was never to get into debt, the second never to raise a mortgage on the property, or to lend to anyone.

Facing the heavy upkeep of the villa with few financial resources, she took, as paying guests, friends and friends of friends. Artists and writers like Tennessee Williams, Roald Dahl and Bertrand Russell climbed those steps in search of peace, relaxation and fun.

'Bertie was delightful, charming and undemanding. But his wife sulked. I guessed that in their little room he was being hen-pecked. I asked him if he would like a separate room. "It would be an unmitigated relief," he said in his precise voice. "She declaims and I am the public meeting."'

Over the years, Daphne had discovered the key to the sometime enigma of Sicilian society. She was anonymously denounced to the authorities for running a *pensione* without the necessary papers. The head of police visited and conceded she should become a *locandieri*, the lowest form of hotel-keeper, which would keep the taxes modest.

Daphne was not the only person to fall in love with Casa Cuseni. There was a trail of suitors but she was always aware of the risks in such relationships.

As she told an English friend: 'So many men want to marry my house. One or two of them wouldn't mind if I came along with it.'

'It is a most marriageable house,' he noted.

To deal with these suitors, she devised strategies that would spare them the sense of rejection. She would tell them she was too independent and thus would make a useless Sicilian wife, or she danced with several different men in one evening, showing she was nothing but a flirt.

Then there was her meeting with Don Ciccio, who told her: '*Signorina*, if there is any individual displeasing you, you have but to let me know.'

She described him as 'quick moving, sunburnt, shabbily dressed. A scar over one eyebrow and drooped eyelid made him hold his head back and up and added to the general impression of ferocious arrogance'.

A nod from him meant she was protected. But she explained this was nothing to do with the Mafia in all its ruthless drug-ridden manifestation.

'Don Ciccio was different. If the state wasn't providing justice, others stepped in.'

Daphne's book is dedicated to Concetta Genio, her beloved housekeeper and friend of many years. 'I would never have been able to save Casa Cuseni without her.'

THIRTY-FOUR

The Compassionate Tourist

I have begun to dread the beginning of the summer season as I know it will generate a flood of emails from anguished tourists who have gone online and found Catsnip. They speak of holidays in various parts of the island that have been disrupted by an encounter with a small cat. What started out as blue skies and sunshine becomes overshadowed by distress and anxiety. It takes me back to my fateful trip in 2002 when Andrew and I stumbled upon Lizzie, setting in motion the chain of events that led to my forming Catsnip. I understand only too well their concern and longing to help in some way. I'd been lucky in finding a friendly vet but then I spoke Italian; apart from the larger towns and cities, it is often difficult to communicate otherwise in Sicily. For those who don't speak Italian, I can imagine their frustration, scanning their phrase books in an attempt to contrive a few sentences. I can picture them in their hotel rooms searching the Internet for animal welfare contacts. I'm in England, they are in Sicily, but at least I can offer advice and put them in touch with someone on the island who may be able to help.

Helen wrote to me from a small tourist town on the western side of the island:

Hello, I found the details of your Catsnip online while searching for an animal charity. I'm currently in Sicily, holidaying in San Vito Lo Capo, and have today found a stray kitten, probably about nine–ten weeks.

I first saw her in the morning and then again later in the afternoon much further into the main town, trying to get into a local supermarket. Everyone ignored her and she seemed so tiny and helpless.

I've brought her back to the apartment we're staying in and have fed and watered her (she was starving), but I was hoping there'd be somewhere that might take her in and rehome her.

I can't find anywhere online so fear the answer is no, but wanted to contact you in case you know of anywhere/body that might help. We're in SVLC until Monday then travelling to Palermo.

I must add here that Helen was on honeymoon when the small feline came into her life but, as she said to me later: 'My husband knew what he was taking on.'

I had never heard of San Vito as I've usually worked on the eastern side of Sicily. That was my first question for Helen.

'San Vito is on the very North West tip of Sicily, west of

Palermo. That's the only way I can describe it really. Nearest big town (other than Palermo) is Trapani. Hope that gives some clue! It's basically a tiny Italian holiday resort,' she emailed.

The moment I saw the word 'Trapani' I knew I had a lead. Remember the story of Dina, the elderly Dalmatian, of Susie and Esther's long car journey from Cefalù to find her? Raimonda, the OIPA volunteer, had filled in the rest of the story. I sent an SOS email asking for her help once more. Meanwhile, I could sense Helen's growing desperation as the hours ticked away. She continued frantically to search the Internet and contacted every lead she found, but with no positive results.

She wrote: 'I have been through my other options which are to appeal to a Canadian-Sicilian lady we met in a cafe yesterday when we first noticed the kitten but she didn't seem that concerned with her at the time. Or to cycle to a vet just outside SVLC to see if they would care for her until she's big enough to fend for herself. Both are long shots. Added complication is that we're staying in a hotel where they aren't very keen on animals, which means we're having to keep her out of view. I'm just dreading a situation where we have to abandon her again come Monday. I've even investigated taking her to Palermo and leaving her with someone there but (a) I can't find anybody/place in Palermo and (b) I imagine Palermo is a much tougher place for a kitten than SVLC. You're right… I feel helpless. And so sad for her.'

By now the kitten had been given a name: Gavroche, after the waif of Victor Hugo's *Les Misérables*. *Oh dear*, I thought, *once you've done that it becomes 'your' kitten rather than just a stray*. Throughout that Thursday, I waited for Raimonda's response, while more emails arrived from Helen.

I'm getting more and more nervous by the hour, as we really only have Friday, Saturday and Sunday to find someone and of course the longer she's with me, the more attached I'm getting. There have been a lot of tears today! And she really is tiny and not very old at all. I don't think she'd fare very well on her own.

I'm going to explore car hire this evening, which will make transporting her a lot easier (slight hitch is that my photo on my licence has expired though, so not sure they'll let me). I have never said a prayer in my life but I will tonight!

By now I was beginning to get as anxious as Helen about the fate of this little scrap. I dreaded how distressed she would be if she had to leave the kitten behind.

Meanwhile, it seemed that there were no romantic dinners à deux on this honeymoon.

I walked into town this evening and spoke again with the lady that owns the cafe where we first saw Gavroche but she wasn't interested in helping though she does have a cat of her own.

I have completely lost hope that anyone in San Vito can help but am now resolute that I will not leave her here. I'd like to get her back to the UK so need to find someone who can look after her for at least a month and who has access to a vet.

I'm going to cycle her up to the local vet in the next town along from us tomorrow morning to see if they can do anything. But if you could also call Raimonda tomorrow I'd be very grateful. Getting very desperate now.

So was I. I sent another message to Raimonda. Suddenly, an image of Dina appeared on the screen. Quickly, I sent Helen an email.

Raimonda has answered tonight and here is what she says:

'To help this kitten you should contact the *vigili urbani* (the municipal police) and tell them that Oipa has been informed of this situation. San Vito has an agreement with a local vet and therefore the kitten should be helped.'

Think this is your best bet. Even if you plan to take this kitten back you need to find somewhere to leave her for the necessary quarantine.

But Helen's reply worried me. She didn't seem to have read my email properly.

I'm taking her to the local vets in Macari this morning in hope they'll care for her in line with their agreement with OIPA. I just hope to God they are true to their word... and that they're open! I'm sure I read somewhere on Wednesday that they open 9.15–1.00 on weekdays, but I now can't find the website I was looking at. To be honest, I'd decided that come Monday I would leave her in a box with a note and some money outside the vets anyway. The thought of just leaving her was making me feel sick.

Later, when we met, she told me: 'I couldn't leave her. I wouldn't have got on the plane; I would have emailed my boss to say I'd be back in the UK later than planned. I even thought of smuggling her onto the flight, but guessed that wouldn't have worked.'

From San Vito, Helen wrote: 'I've asked my hotel to order a taxi for 10am so I'll let you know. Just need to find a box to carry her in now.'

'True to Sicilian hospitality,' Helen told me when we met, 'the owner of the hotel dismissed the idea of a taxi and said his son would drive us wherever we wanted to go.

'At first he didn't understand we wanted to go to the vet, until he saw Gavroche in the box. He looked pretty surprised.'

But the vet wasn't there: Helen was told she would be back on Saturday.

'This is really worrying for me because if the vet is not there tomorrow, or will not take her, then I have very little time left to help her. We go to Palermo on Monday and fly to England on Tuesday and do not have a car.

'To add to the complication, now that the hotel knows we have Gavroche they have forbidden me from letting her in the room,' she emailed.

I sent her a very concise email: 'Take Raimonda's advice and go to the municipal police. They are in touch with OIPA and will know where you should take the kitten. You can call Raimonda if necessary because she does speak a bit of English. You have the number, don't you?'

It was by now Saturday and I was out during the day but always at the back of my mind was how Helen was getting on. The moment I arrived home I switched on my computer, once again dreading that Helen had been disappointed. What I read surpassed anything I had hoped for.

'Hello. So some good news, I think. We took her to the police station in San Vito. When we arrived they said, "No cats, no cats!" I'm a woman with a career but I know how to become a helpless female when the occasion arises,' she told me. 'I sat on the floor of the police station and burst into tears. This did the trick and they fetched an officer who could speak a little English. I showed him Raimonda's email and we telephoned her.'

Because of the language problem what happened next was surreal. Helen and her husband found themselves in a police car, presumably to go to a vet.

'Instead they stopped just down the road outside a private house. A woman came out, holding back a barking dog, and Gavroche was whisked away.'

As Helen related: 'I felt bewildered. We went on the beach for a couple of hours and I tried to read but just couldn't concentrate. "We've just handed her over without knowing anything about what will happen to her," I cried to my husband. Eventually, he agreed we should go and knock on the woman's door. She greeted us warmly and invited us in to see the kitten. Gavroche was sitting in an armchair in the living room like the Queen of Sheba.

'The lady's name is Antonella Siino and with broken English/Italiano and un poco de Español we worked out that this nice lady is a volunteer with OIPA and that her dog is also a rescue. She often fosters animals but she had decided to adopt Gavroche, whom she has renamed Londres, in our honour. I simply couldn't be happier that she is safe and well and being cared for by someone who is so obviously an animal lover.

'None of this could have happened without you and Raimonda – thank you from the bottom of my heart! At times I felt like I was mad for caring so much, but you confirmed others care too. And now I'm going to go outside and enjoy the Sicilian sunshine with my husband, who I've barely spoken to over the past forty-eight hours.'

A week or so later, another email arrived from Sicily.

Hi, on holiday in Castiglione di Sicilia and my wife has found a helpless tiny kitten (feral, obviously and without its mother). Can you help with locating a home or a vet for it please?

Had they checked the mother wasn't in the neighbourhood? I queried. My sister had just returned from Spain, where two kittens had turned up at their apartment. She fed them for two days and lay awake at night, wondering what would happen to them when the family left.

'I prayed the mother would turn up the following day,' she told me. 'Then, I was looking out across the fields behind the apartment and I'm sure I saw her. The kittens didn't return again.'

But Michael replied swiftly that they didn't think there was a mother around. He seemed to be a lost soul, crying all last night and trying everyone's affections that afternoon.

Doubt he has an owner – more like, as with other cats, he owns several humans!

OK, could they give me some idea as to where Castiglione di Sicilia was in relation to, say, Giardini Naxos/Taormina? 'I think you are nearer to the eastern side of the island?'

'We are about forty-five minutes from Taormina, and certain the mother is not around, it was crying all last night. We leave this Sunday (my wife would take her home if she could!)' came the reply.

That evening I called them on their mobile. Michael sounded calm but Susan was very emotional. I told them about Qua La Zampa, the pet shop where, last year, Angela and Marco had cared for Lucky Star until a home could be found for her.

Later, Michael emailed: 'Piccolino has been smuggled back into our room tonight, and we will take him to Taormina in the morning. Hopefully we can leave him there. The vet gave him a clean bill of health (I tried to explain to my wife that he was a street cat and therefore a little scrawny). Anyhow, he has just had the best part of half a tin of Royal Canin and is now exploring.'

The following morning, I called the pet shop. Angela wasn't there but I spoke to Marco. He sounded very gloomy: Taormina was a chaos where cats were concerned. They were left outside the shop every day; he had six already. They could board Piccolino for a few days but couldn't commit to homing him.

I related the news to Michael. In the background I could hear Susan saying that perhaps the best thing to do would be to take the kitten back to the vet and have him put to sleep.

I reacted strongly: 'These feral cats are tough. As you say, they do look scrawny but they survive. There will be some elderly woman in the area who feed them. Why put a healthy little cat to sleep?'

I was reminded of E.M. Forster's novel *Where Angels Fear to Tread*, of well-meaning visitors unversed in another culture, who create mayhem and tragedy. Though I could understand their distress, I asked myself yet again, *Was it really wise to take in a small feline when you knew that, in a few days, you had to leave?* What did you think would happen to it? This wasn't Britain with shelters and animal welfare associations; it was a country that for the most part did not care for cats. What was worse was the notion of having a healthy animal put to sleep because you thought it was 'best' for it.

Meanwhile, Michael came back to me. They had contacted my lovely vet, Oscar La Manna, and taken Piccolino to his surgery, where it was found he was 'suffering from every parasite know to cat kind: roundworms, fleas etc.'. Oscar believed there was someone who wanted a small cat and would collect it the next day. Later came news that Luigi had not turned up.

'Don't know what we will do if he is not collected,' Michael wrote. 'Hopefully Oscar will be true to his word and find a caring home – he cannot go onto the streets as he is too small to fend for himself.'

I felt defeated but was delighted when, a day or so later, Oscar contacted me.

'We've had some difficulties with the little Piccolino because, as you well know, here in Sicily there isn't a good culture where animals are concerned. There are no shelters or reception centres for ferals. The authorities speak constantly of helping animals but they don't spend one coin to look after them. This is a very beautiful place but its inhabitants are too egoistical and stupid. Luckily, there are we vets who are freelance and give a hand at our expense to these poor little feral animals that need treatment. The state doesn't help, only profits from our sensibility. Thus I have decided to keep this little cat and look after it until I can find someone to give it a home.'

Not all these stories have such satisfactory endings. Some are left unfinished and continue to nag.

Dawn contacted me, wondering if anything could be done to help a small sick cat: 'The poor creature has scratched itself bald in places and sits hunched up with its tongue hanging partially out and drooling a small amount of yellow/pink-brown liquid. It seems to be obtaining food from inside the gate of the local residence where two other healthy cats live but now seems to be shut outside and looks in a bad state.'

The couple went to nearby Qua La Zampa and tried to make themselves understood, using a pre-recording on a translation app. However, as Dawn said: 'We didn't get very far due to the language barrier but the lady seemed to be pointing us in the direction of the Corso and mentioned the police. I bought a couple of pouches and the cat has eaten one, this evening.'

On my advice, they called Oscar La Manna. He told them he would come out to check on the cat if they could capture it.

Later, when I talked to Dawn, she said: 'We were both very tired after a difficult year and this was supposed to be a relaxing holiday but we ended up worrying about Lionel, as I called him, most of the time.'

Although Lionel seemed quite friendly, she doubted if she could catch him without a cat carrier. They had planned a trip to Etna the following day, so I told them, meanwhile, I would call a friend, one of the rarer *gattaro* (or cat men).

Carmelo runs a garage backing onto a yard that throngs with cats. He is a dedicated cat lover and spends much of his salary on feeding and caring for them. Yes, he said, if the couple came round in the early evening, they could certainly borrow a carrier.

My plan failed. Returned from Etna, Dawn and her boyfriend were ravenous and went for a meal before negotiating the dark roads to the garage. They were too late: Carmelo had shut the garage and gone home.

Time was now running out, for the couple were due to leave a day later. They had been keeping an eye on the house where the cats roamed and noticed a woman coming and going.

'We are unsure of her involvement and have not previously approached her, as we didn't know whether we would be able to communicate.'

They were feeling confused because of this problem with language. Did the woman own Lionel or was he sneaking in to feed with the other two, healthy-looking cats? Meanwhile,

Oscar was standing by for their call. I explained the situation to him and sent Dawn his reply.

'These are Oscar's thoughts: if the cat is sick and is a feral it needs care. Even if someone feeds it they would be happy that it was being given treatment.'

She remained unconvinced. 'I would prefer to know whether the lady owns the cat before we proceed, as I am still worried about a confrontation and nobody being available to interpret in the event. I am also conscious the time is ticking by and not sure how long Oscar will be available now. Would he be available tomorrow, if necessary?'

In the end, they were faced by the situation I know so well, that of having to pack up and leave with the question hanging over them: what will happen to that cat now?

Sure enough, Dawn continued to agonise over Lionel after her return to England: 'I have felt so helpless concerning Lionel, as I called him. I just wish it would have been possible for someone to have called over and assisted us in getting an expert opinion with a view to making him more comfortable. I feel so sad for him, but realise his case is just the tip of the iceberg. He was there on the step yesterday evening as usual at about 5pm and we gave him a pouch, which he gobbled down. We saw him again on the step at 11pm when we returned from the town centre, which was to be the last time – he wasn't there this morning to give him a pouch, as planned. It is hard not to think about him and it makes me realise how lucky Kenny is – it is lovely to have him home.'

I, too, found it difficult to get the image of Lionel out of my mind. So I racked my brains and finally contacted

Eleanor, an English friend and *gattara* who lives in Taormina and looks after twenty cats of her own. Could she find time to go along and clarify things? She promised to do her best and later wrote to me:

Yesterday afternoon I finally managed to locate Lionel, sitting in a plant pot in the garden at 23a Dietro Cappuccini, looking rather poorly. I guessed he was probably getting fed by the owners, seeing as he was sitting in there, behind the fence. I wanted to speak to the owners to ask if he was their cat, but didn't know which bell to ring.

Luckily, I met Chiara, who lives in the same street and she said she knows you. She told me that the people who live in that house are nice and also animal lovers, and kindly volunteered to come with me to enquire.

We spoke to a nice gentleman who confirmed that Lionel is a stray and said that his father feeds him. I explained that Dawn wanted to help Lionel and has given a donation for veterinary fees, but he told me that Lionel has already been seen by a vet. He said that Lionel has had bad dysentery, and that is why he is so thin and has his tongue sticking out. Apparently, he is being given some pills for it, but he looked like he desperately needed to be on a drip to me.

Now I don't know what to think or do. To be honest, Jenny, Lionel looked to me to be on his last legs. The man spoke of bad dysentery and him having had bad diarrhoea, but I think it's due to something else, probably some organ failure. I've seen nearly all of my cats that have passed away go the same way.

I could organise trying to capture Lionel and get him to Oscar, but I don't really know if it's worth it. In these circumstances, any vet will do blood analysis and at best maybe diagnose kidney failure. They will keep the animal in a cage for therapy, which is very expensive and the animal usually dies anyway. I think it's an unpleasant end, especially for a feral cat who isn't used to being indoors in a strange chemically-smelling environment.

I asked the lady if they wouldn't like a second opinion on Lionel, especially seeing as the costs would be covered by Catsnip, but they seemed convinced that Lionel was being taken care of and is being given something for his condition.

And there I had to leave the story of Lionel. There is a limit to how much we outsiders can interfere. However, I am grateful to Helen, Michael, Susan and Dawn for stopping to help these creatures instead of just walking away.

As Oscar La Manna said later: 'It is fortunate that there are these animal lovers who give a hand and try to help these feral animals, taking them to us vets who cooperate by giving them the right treatment at a ridiculously low price.'

I've known Oscar for a year, but only comparatively recently have I realised what a truly remarkable and almost unique Sicilian vet he is. How did he become a vet, I asked him, and how does he deal with the general attitudes towards animals in Sicily?

'Ever since I was a boy I had a passion for every kind

of animal, including insects that I loved to touch. Once, I brought an entire ants' nest into the house. Thus, when I grew up, I chose to become a vet and, if I had that choice again, I would do it a thousand times over.

'However, after twenty years of working in the field here, I feel under-valued and limited in what I can do. I have discovered many things but the first and enormous lesson I have learned is that more than 50 per cent of animal owners in Sicily are ignorant and a threat to their animals because, at the very first hurdle, particularly economic, they are ready to abandon them. It would need the vet's presence in schools to teach children that animals merit respect; they are not toys that one can throw away, they are living beings that need caring for, even if it turns out to be expensive. Thus, those who know they can't afford it should never take on an animal because it will put the two of them at risk.

'If one doesn't have an income, it is necessary to be objective and not endanger the life of a companion animal – much better never to bring one into the house.

'Unfortunately, civilisation will never arrive here, the people are too stupid and convinced they are right and teach their own children this erroneous stupidity and egoism.

'In your country, England, things are very different – there is order, services, much more civilisation.

'Here, there is nothing left for me but to fight this infinite ignorance in order to defend these defenceless little animals from the cruel hands of men who are uncivilised and egoistic.'

As Oscar has said to me: 'It is fortunate for the feral cats that at least some of us freelance vets are concerned about them and at our own expense take care of them.'

The volunteers of OIPA I've mentioned several times before are another dedicated team of animal lovers, scattered across Sicily. Then there are people like Valeria Cundari and her volunteers at the ARCA refuge, overflowing with unwanted animals. Their daily battle is horrendous; fighting ignorance and downright cruelty, trying to cope with the over-population of cats and dogs. How they would welcome the very different approach of Trieste in Northern Italy.

THIRTY-FIVE

The Cat Sanctuaries of Trieste

The city where James Joyce once lived and wrote has two complementary cat shelters that many local people trust, admire and support. Il Gattile is a safe haven for needy and ailing cats. Located in the city centre just behind the courthouse, it was formerly one of Trieste's old houses, which always had interior courtyards; one wall is actually shared with the city's jailhouse. Since 1992, Il Gattile has welcomed many cats from feral colonies, a daily duty for the volunteers who tirelessly dedicate their lives to these needy animals. Many of the felines are found in the street in a very bad condition, others are abandoned and left to this vagabond life.

At L'oasis Felina on the outskirts of the city, 155 cats roam happily and undisturbed in an enclosed and protected green space. Unless they are adopted and go to loving homes, they will live out their lives here in peace. When cat colonies are displaced because of construction work, they can be relocated here.

I first heard about this animal-friendly city when I contacted Kathy via her website, catsinitaly, for possible help with Helen's foundling kitten. She was quick to respond, although, happily, little Gavroche found a kindly home. An American-Asian, Kathy has lived in Italy for many years with her Italian husband, Giorgio.

As she told me, the veterinary school in Vienna is the oldest in Europe, and Trieste, close to the Austrian border, is very much influenced by the Austro-Hapsburg attitudes where animals are concerned. The tradition of caring for animals goes back a long way. Since the early 1900s, for example, it has been obligatory to provide bowls of water outside shops for animals to drink from.

Kathy related the story of her life with cats and how she became involved with them. She met Giorgio at university in the States and, later, they moved abroad. As an engineer he has been posted to various parts of Italy. It wasn't until they arrived in Trieste in 2008 that she became a volunteer at Il Gattile.

'I guess I was a normal person until then,' she laughed. 'I had never worked with animals in my life before. I just had two cats, now they have taken over my life.'

'I have two special wards at present: a twenty-year-old colony cat who is blind and deaf. She's had her cage door open now for ten days, but hasn't come out by herself yet. I work with her senses of smell and touch; she loves fresh sardine fillets and I let her know I'm there by tapping on the cage floor so she can feel the vibrations. I don't touch her, not yet. Today at noon, you should have seen her come out of her curled-up lethargy when she smelled the fish!

'My other feral ward was thought to be an aggressive spitty meany; he's just a timid, fearful, streetwise cat. This un-neutered tom came in with an open abscess on the whole of his left cheek; he'd been living out in the park for about a year like that. The *gattara* tried to trap him, unsuccessfully, three or four times during the course of the year. Eventually, Magna was brought in at the end of March. He still has about a month to go with his therapy. We recently let him free in the room and he lived, terrified, for ten days under the cages. So I put him back in a luxury top-floor (third cage up), with views out to the sunny courtyard and views through the glass door, where he watches our ninety or so cats go up and down the stairs to the attic living quarters.

'When he first arrived, he was very hissy and angry. It took me ten days before he was eating out of my hand. On the way back from a few days at the vets for laser therapy, he was still anesthetised, I coo-ed while walking back to Il Gattile. Once back, I stroked the length of his body several times; that was to leave my smell on him. Sure enough, the next day he looked at me differently – with recognition? With warmth? Affectionately? And I hadn't opened the can of salmon cat food yet.

'I didn't see him for a week, and at noon I went up on the stepladder to his cage and he was fine with me entering his space. And he ate some sardine fillets from my fingers.'

This cattery is obviously a hive of activity. Some of Kathy's special duties are keeping the admission/release information up to date for the sick cats (twenty-four cages). Spay/neuter campaign and adoption records are kept separately by another volunteer (twenty-six cages).

'I do one cleaning shift a week, this entails making sure volunteers will be present, usually about five or six. I also deal with adoptions, field telephone calls, handle emergencies and receive visitors and donors at the door.

'I maintain the Facebook page and website, and provide a lot of the photos and graphics work. My work with cat handling involves transferring from trap to cage and vice versa, cleaning cages which house cats that are extremely feral and those with special needs, such as bone fractures.

'I foster feral kittens in my home; summer in Italy is the time when we rescue so many of them. Having spent three weeks in my foster guest-room, three kittens went to their new home, last night. Whew! And the remaining two brothers will be going to the cat sanctuary. I have just taken them down for the weekend to Il Gattile, where I volunteer. Who knows, the perfect people might wander in? If not, they will have a lovely, protected garden where they will mix with other cats and kittens. I help in the decision of whether they'd be happier if people adopt them or living at the cat sanctuary. Rarely and if they're big enough, I may be able to convince the *gattara/o* to take them back in their particular feline colony.'

The tranquil lives of these cats, so lovingly cared for, is currently threatened by the town hall's decision to relocate the fruit and vegetable market onto land occupied by the sanctuary. This news swiftly mobilised the entire district of Borgo San Sergio, its neighbourhood committee comprising the local residents, campers from the also threatened site, and the volunteers of Il Gattile. They have launched an online petition asking town councillors and the mayor to change their plan. This followed a town hall announcement that the sanctuary would be moved to an adequate neighbouring area, but the volunteers remain concerned. How can such a transfer be effected? And above all, why pollute this green space, with traffic coming and going, noise and refuse from the market?

In sharp contrast to the often contempt with which the *gattare* are viewed in Sicily, Trieste honours them. Every year, the Il Gattile Association awards a prize to a woman, acknowledging her work in rescuing and caring for feral cats. The award was instituted in 2001 to celebrate the birthday of Margherita Hack, a prime mover in the foundation of Il Gattile. In 2014, it was given not to a *gattara* but to the threatened L'oasis Felina, the space that Margherita loved so much, during her lifetime.

THIRTY-SIX

Sadie, Katarina and the Incredible Rescue of a Blind Kitten

*T*his is the story of Katarina, of how a small Sicilian cat brought Catsnip, Oscar and Elke together, to the rescue. Above all, it is the story of Sadie and her determination to save the blind feline.

Francavilla is a typical small Sicilian town, approximately ten miles inland from the coastal resort of Taormina, with spectacular views. Although much of the town is now fairly modern, you can still see signs of former times, with the ruins of the one-time castle overlooking the inhabitants, and the old winding streets that evoke images of its medieval past. Nearby is the famous Alcantara Gorge, where an impressive torrent of water rushes below vertical lava cliffs. Located on the north slopes of Mount Etna, the river is one of the few in Sicily that flows year round. Several thousand years ago, its path was blocked by a large lava flow from the volcano's slopes. The cold water quickly cooled the lava, which resulted in its crystallising and forming the unique rocky columns. Over the next few thousand years, the river carved a path through those columns and resulted in the gorge.

If you like to explore, there are numerous trails where you can hike along the top of the gorge. And if you are looking to cool off, you can relax at Gorge Beach. The easy way to get down into the gorge is to take the lift; for the more adventurous there are stairs. There is a gorge trail that follows the river upstream and offers wonderful views from the top. It takes you through the botanical gardens and citrus groves, where you can sit and stare. Here you can gaze into the heart of the gorge and the waterfalls from the beach, so don't be afraid to explore. The water is advertised as being cold but in the heat of the summer it is very refreshing. No wonder it is a popular spot with locals during the scorching Sicilian summers.

Sadie and her boyfriend Eddie had arrived here to stay for a night or two on a farm, the so-called *agriturismo*. From the 1950s and continuing through the 1970s, small-scale farming in Italy came under threat. Many farmers abandoned their land to search for work in larger towns. But Italians value highly the traditions and produce of small-scale food manufacturers, and, by 1985, a law was passed defining *agriturismo*. Many abandoned buildings and estates were restored, some for holiday homes, and many for this kind of tourism. It allowed the small farmer to augment the income from the farm, and for holidaymakers to sample the bounty of a rural life in Italy.

It all seemed idyllic and very relaxing until the couple noticed that one of the farm cats seemed to be bumping into things and falling down steps.

In July 2014, Sadie and Eddie were on a road trip in Sicily when they first met Katarina. Sadie recalled: 'We had stopped overnight at a farm in the mountains about five miles from the nearest town. Kat walked into our apartment outhouse door, literally. She then fell down the steps and tried again to navigate the door.

'At that point I didn't realise that she was totally blind, but it was clear she was struggling. One of her eyes was protruding dangerously out of the socket, and the other was opaque and deformed. She was a mess and I was horrified by the gruesome state of her face. Her tabby fur was matted and she was worryingly thin and fragile. I distinctly remember her stumbling and falling down two or three stairs in such a pitiful way that made me think she was beyond help. I would have rather been responsible for ending her life than to leave her stumbling frantically around in darkness, searching for crumbs.

'To my surprise, she was remarkably affectionate, trusting and confident, and quite boldly came into our room demanding food. She didn't appear to be fearful, of anything or anyone. She had a sort of brazen confidence, despite the fact that she was at such a disadvantage. She purred when I stroked her and was happy to be picked up and cuddled. All of the other feral cats kept their distance and hissed when you attempted to approach them.

'She slept outside our door that night and greeted us in the morning. We stayed for two more nights at that farm and the cat stayed with us, sleeping outside alone on a chair. She seemed very vulnerable out there, curled up around herself, ants crawling around her face and with local dogs patrolling the area.

'It was then that I contacted Catsnip to get some advice and enquire about a local vet. I didn't realise at that point to what extent I would have to commit to this little cat and how many people would become instrumental in her journey.'

It was that summer of 2014 when I first heard from Sadie: 'I have found a stray kitten, which has something wrong with her eyes. I believe she is blind and suffering. One eye seems to be missing but I'm not sure, as she is a mess. If this is something that she can be helped with, I would like to bring her back to the UK. However, I am really struggling to find ways to fly her back with me. She is very young and friendly; just arrived in our bedroom and will not leave.'

I gave her Oscar La Manna's telephone number and he suggested they take the cat to his surgery, which raised the first dilemma: Sadie and Eddie were due to leave the following day. We conferred on the phone.

Said Sadie: 'The only thing we can do is to drive through on our way to Syracuse and drop her off at around 11.30am. My concern is that I would be placing responsibility on Oscar, and then leaving – however, if you believe that the cat will be cared for, we will keep her inside and definitely bring her tomorrow. I am afraid that she will need hefty medical attention, and that I will not be around to administer that. If the cat can be saved, then I am willing to make arrangements to bring her to London and have her live her life with us.'

Sadie called Oscar and made valiant attempts to explain all this but, as she said, it might have been lost in translation. However, she wasn't going to give up.

'We have fallen a bit in love with her. If he is willing to do all required medical treatment, microchipping and blood-work, I will do whatever needed to get her to London safely and quickly. Or, if he believes it would be better, he could take her back to the farm where she lives, but these are both big asks to a total stranger and it's difficult to communicate with him as my Italian is terrible.'

The cat had now firmly ensconced herself with her new admirers and was tucking in to unaccustomed goodies, although Sadie was still very concerned about the state of one of her eyes. It seemed to her it would have to be removed.

As she relates: 'So, with Kat in a box, and the Italian farmers looking very bemused as to my apparent kidnapping of a blind feral cat, we drove to the local vet, who was fantastically kind and understanding.'

Indeed, on that Friday morning, I imagined the surprise of their hosts as Sadie and Eddie loaded the little cat into their car. Later, I had a call from the surgery: Sadie was again struggling with her Italian and asked if I could speak to Oscar. I could hear Eddie's voice in the background and there seemed to be a problem. Briefly, Oscar explained that to treat the cat and do all the necessary preparation to obtain her pet passport would cost around 1,000 euros. Sadie and Eddie were taken aback; they had never envisaged it would cost so much and didn't have that kind of money with them.

Oscar came back on the phone. The vet sounded baffled.

So now what was to happen to the cat? She certainly needed an operation.

We agreed they would pay for this and I would send a donation to cover some of the rest of her treatment. The cat's future was left in the balance.

Back home in London, Sadie couldn't put 'her' Sicilian cat out of her mind. How would the blind feline manage if she were returned to the farm? And what was the alternative? She tormented herself thinking about the little cat's future, as did I. What was to happen next?

Wrote Sadie:

I can let Oscar know the exact location where I found her, but I do not think the hotel owners will feed her. They are not hostile – but they do not want to encourage the cats further, and were quite delighted, if not a little bemused, at me taking her with me! All the cats at this property looked reasonably healthy, and I imagine that they survive on scraps from the kitchen and food given to them by the guests – but of course with her blindness, I do not feel rested or confident on the subject. The other option is that she be rehomed, which unless Oscar knows of someone who would be willing to care for her for the rest of her life (which may be lengthy), it looks like it would mean that she come to us in London. We live in a large ground-floor flat with several steps down to a very large, enclosed private garden. There is no nearby access to a road, which is a plus. I would want to teach her to use a cat-flap as I think it's important for cats to access outside space, sounds, smells (especially given her blindness). I have read up a bit about blind cats and understand that they can cope well, and be happy.

At that point neither Sadie nor I realised what this decision would involve. I was also pondering whether bringing the cat to England was the best plan. How feral was she? Yes, Sadie had said she was affectionate but how strong were her links to her territory on the farm and her bonding with the other cats? Sadie had also told me she had a companion cat. How important was this to her?

I pointed this out: 'I think you have done something wonderful in allowing this cat to have treatment and am transferring funds to Oscar's account, this evening, but perhaps it would be better for her to return to her companions there. Cats can cope with blindness more than we could.'

But Sadie couldn't forget that the cat had 'found' them, turning up in their room and not wanting to leave: 'She is so very affectionate with humans and, after observing her, she seemed fairly irritated by the younger cats. She appeared to be far more human-orientated. However, I want to do the best for her so am happy to take that advice.'

She told me she already had a rescue dog and I raised this with her. Would this be a problem for a blind cat?

Sadie came back to me quickly:

My dog, Thelma, is a medium size mix-breed with a very sweet temperament. She adores cats and would be very, very delighted by an addition. She is still a young dog and is not averse to chasing the neighbours' cats, but we have lived with cats before now and she likes them.

Having seen this little cat interact with the two farm dogs (one naughty puppy), I do not doubt that she can hold her own. She was not scared of them, and tactfully warned them away when they got too close. They all seemed to live quite harmoniously together, but as you say, she was definitely at a disadvantage and it broke my heart to see her fall down steps and walk into walls. That said, she didn't seem unhappy.

So these are my honest concerns. Having spent time with the cat, she was very quick to purr and happy to sit on laps and be cuddled, but I understand that the familiarity of her old home and possible companion might be very important for her. I started the process and will not abandon it either way.

After some discussion and persuasion, the inevitable was decided. Katarina was totally blind and therefore even after emergency treatment for her eyes, morally, she could not be returned to the farm, where she would starve to death, if she was not eaten by a predator first. Nor was there a rescue option in Sicily. She was in limbo at the vets, in a cage, as Sadie and Eddie had to return to London. Katarina was homeless, now clocking up a massive bill at the vets, and requiring his very dedicated team to intensively treat her and quarantine her during the summer holidays.

Said Sadie: 'It was my naivety that had brought her to a place that now required my decision about her future. It was my duty, I felt, to see the process through to some conclusion, and this sweet little cat deserved a home. My boyfriend was less than impressed by the scenario, understandably. We had just moved into a new house and already had a large, extremely messy young dog to contend with at home. The last thing he wanted was a severely disabled Sicilian cat. We had no idea what she was or wasn't capable of.'

It was now clear to me that Sadie's heart was set on giving the cat a loving home. She had a week's holiday towards the end of August and could fly to Sicily, complete the necessary documents and bring Katarina home with her. Who was I to stand in her way? It was time to look into practicalities and here we found it was not going to be a simple process.

In the past, if you wanted to bring an animal into the UK, it would have to stay in quarantine for six months. This cost the owners a lot of money, not to mention the distress of being separated from their pets for such a long time. Fairly recently, the rules have been relaxed, making it somewhat easier. As long as the cat or dog has been microchipped and vaccinated against rabies, they can be issued with a pet passport. After a 21-day wait, they may travel freely within countries. The rules of the UK are still stricter than those for the rest of Europe, too strict in some people's opinion. On the other hand, there has been no reported case of rabies in the UK since 1902.

My thoughts went to Oscar, who had sent me photographs of Katarina post-operation and had so kindly agreed to keep her in the surgery until Sadie could make her arrangements. It seemed that he had fallen in love with her too.

He wrote to me: 'I think that this cat is really special and I too want the best for her. The most beautiful arrangement is Sadie's house seeing that it was she who found the cat and sought to save her from the streets. Thus I agree that she should take her to England so that she can have the best possible care. I have already told Sadie that the cost enabling her to take the cat home is 100 euros and includes microchip, anti-rabies inoculation, de-worming, three certificates and phials of flea treatment. For the days during which I keep the cat until collected, with all the medical care she will need, I will accept whatever contribution she cares to give me.'

It was now August and Oscar was officially on holiday, although going in each day to care for Katarina. I felt uncomfortable with all the trouble I was putting him to. After all, it was I who had first put these wheels in motion.

He wrote: 'I need to know with certainty the day in which Sadie wishes to come here. She will have to stay for several days to organise the documents because she has to go to the Veterinary Office in Taormina to sign them. I will do my best to make it all as easy as possible. The cat is very well, eating and is much more calm now that she has been neutered. Let me know when Sadie plans to come.'

A day or so later, he wrote: 'She is an angel, a very special cat who deserves a special home.'

This was exactly what Sadie was preparing – she told me she was building a ramp so the cat could easily access the stairs!

'Eddie is now quite amused by the whole scenario and is helping me make arrangements. I can finance her coming here and have started raising considerable funds. I work for a children's charity so that comes as second nature. I have some big sponsors in my contacts, so who knows? I want to look after the Gatta Trovatella!'

And I wanted to help her but I was still concerned about a blind cat travelling such a distance. I remembered Elke telling me about the plane and train journeys she made with her four cats. They had always travelled with her in the cabin when she went from Sicily to Rome and also to Germany. I knew the reassurance my cat Sheba needed on journeys and was comforted that Sadie would be by her side. Then I discovered, once again, British rules were different: animals had to travel as live cargo. There were no exceptions for blind cats like Katarina. Oh dear, how would she cope with that? Would she be traumatised by the noise and movement? Oscar also expressed his concerns. This was becoming more stressful by the day.

Sadie was also encountering difficulties. She wrote: 'I'm really struggling to find an airline that will take the cat. Alitalia do NOT bring animals into the UK anymore and BA has a strict policy which does not permit animals in the cabin. It will cost several hundred to book her in cargo. This airline seems to fly directly to London, which is one saving grace. Airlines are generally useless, have no info online and are unhelpful.'

We were moving through August, Katarina had been with Oscar for almost a month. She was thriving on all the care and attention he was giving her but she couldn't stay there forever. Sadie continued to struggle with the logistics of getting the little feline into the UK. I was still concerned about her having to travel as live cargo and so I consulted Elke.

'It does seem so complicated compared with the rest of Europe,' she agreed. 'And I understand Sadie being daunted by all this paperwork. Tell her to call me the moment she arrives in Taormina and I'll go with her to the Veterinary Office and translate so that she can complete the documents.'

One afternoon Elke called on Oscar and the two of them got on like a house on fire.

'La Manna is a lovely person and remember Sicilians are very accustomed to problems. I went ice-cream eating with him today and we had lots of laughs.'

Meanwhile, Sadie remained concerned. She had been double-checking the UK regulations for a pet passport and wanted to be certain everything was in place: 'I don't want to be turned back at the border or, worse, for Kat to have to go into quarantine. The microchip has to be placed before the anti-rabies vaccination. I am also concerned that Oscar hasn't factored in the 21-day waiting period.'

I was now in conflict. On the one hand, I wanted this transfer to go smoothly and without hitch. On the other, I disliked having to continually bother Oscar, who was still on holiday. I kept on apologising to him.

Things suddenly came to a head when Sadie said she had to confirm flights by nine o'clock that Thursday evening. It was now crucial, she said, to have all her queries clearly answered. I waited for Oscar to reply. *It must be a wonderfully sunny day in Sicily*, I told myself. *Who knew, maybe he was on the beach!* However, at four that afternoon, I was able to text Sadie that all was in place.

I heard nothing over that Bank Holiday weekend but I had my own concerns, trying to make important appointments in France, where I was shortly to present my new novel. I just presumed all had gone to plan and wondered when Sadie would go to the surgery to be reunited with Katarina.

Then I heard that Sadie, faced with all these difficulties, had been trying to find another option: 'This is not a simple process of me coming over. I would have to fly over (based on when her 21-day period is over), stay in Taormina as I can't drive, collect and sign documents from somewhere, travel to Giardini Naxos on public transport, collect the cat and get a train/bus to Catania, fly to Rome with her, then transfer her to another flight in cargo.'

That's when the bureaucratic nightmare to bring her to the UK began: 'Sicily it seems has its own way of operating, and there are various nonsensical hoops that make the process extremely costly and slow. The language barrier was also very taxing. However, with the help of Catsnip, locals in Sicily, the vet and an agency in Rome, Kat eventually arrived at our home in London… that's cutting a very long story short and eclipsing six weeks of constant organisation and changes in the plan, as new rules and blockades became apparent. At one point it seemed that the only way to get the cat to the airport for 7am, for the only flight that would accept her (a flight which was not even going to London), would be for an elderly Sicilian removal van driver to be conscripted into the plan,' explained Sadie.

It was certainly complex and she had decided that it would be simpler to use the specialist agency Relocat.

'They can do everything, and advise Oscar, which seems to make more sense than me trying to do this, via you,' said Sadie. 'The plan is that Kat will need to be taken to Catania airport, flown to Rome, stay over a night there, then fly to London the following day!! It is the only way. I hope it will not be too traumatic for her. She will have a strange few hours in transport, but will then be home, and safe. The whole experience is very strange for her, the vets, transport, a new home, a dog, etc. But she is a very young cat, who seems robust enough to cope. After her travels here, she will not be uprooted again, and will have a luxurious life!'

Her other life options were dire.

At this point another player in this drama came on the scene. Mark contacted me from the Rome agency, telling me he would take care of all arrangements from drop-off at Catania airport to delivery to Sadie's London home.

He said: 'I don't think there's any sense in Sadie (who doesn't speak Italian) coming down merely to rent a car/cab and drive for forty minutes from Taormina to Catania. I am arranging two flights, AZ 1710 and BA 547. Live animals must travel as AVI Manifest Cargo to the UK under the Pet Travel Scheme. I won't be able to book flights until I have copies of pet passport pages.'

In Taormina, Elke was standing by:

Tomorrow morning I will go with La Manna to get the passport of Katarina. I have the appointment at 1pm in that health office. La Manna and the vet of ASL know precisely what they have to do. After that, I will scan the passport and email it to Mark. He also gave me the exact measurements for the transport-basket, which I will buy, together with a little water distributor.

I have to be at Catania airport at 7.30am. The cat

will take the Alitalia flight to Rome at 10am. Mark will pick her up and put her on the next British Airways flight. So the cat will arrive at Heathrow around 4.00pm that same day, where Sadie has to pick her up and bring her to her new home. This way I think it is perfect and not too stressy at all for Katarina. I will let you know as soon as Mark has told me the exact travelling day, which will not be before 4 or 5 of September. Katarina can stay at La Manna's office, she has completely adapted to the place and he will not ask for any extra money. I will pick her up in the evening before travelling and keep her with me that night because we have to leave here in Taormina at 6.00am to be punctually at the airport.

I have found that all this is being done very professionally by everybody, and I myself are doing this whole fatigue deliberately, because I like animals more than people – ha ha!

I will tell Mark on the phone that Katarina is a very calm cat and does not need tranquillisers. Please, Sadie, can you mail your name and address to me or La Manna again today; he wants to compare it with the one he already has before going to the ASL tomorrow. I hope that everything is clear now and I wish you good luck with Katarina.

I am still trying to find the right transport-cage. Even that has 'special rules'. I cannot believe how complicated it is to ship a cat from Italy to England. Meanwhile, the cat is doing brilliantly.

After a long search Elke finally found the right transportation basket, which conformed to both airlines' requirements, and was awaiting news from Mark on the date of the flights.

It was now September and I was standing in the magnificent gardens of Claude Monet in Giverny, Normandy when Sadie's triumphant email arrived:

> Kat arrived very late last night. She is absolutely lovely. She is in our bedroom and conservatory, just so that she gets used to that part of the house first. She is using her litter tray (she is very clean). She had fresh salmon for dinner and ate biscuits and a little meat this morning!
>
> She certainly can jump! She slept in her little cat bed for an hour and then arrived on our bed and slept cuddled up on my pillow, purring. I'm surprised by how well she gets around, actually. She is very curious, and affectionate. She kept us awake all night purring and trying to sleep on our heads. Maybe she remembers us…

Over the following weeks, Sadie kept me posted: 'Katarina is very cuddly and is quite playful. She hunts and plays based on movement and sound – I think that she is a very clever cat. She is quite fearless.'

A day or so later, the photographs arrived. They showed an adorable and contented Katarina and brought tears to my eyes.

Sadie's most recent email told me: 'She is now a healthy, happy eighteen-month-old cat, who not only circumnavigates around our home with ease, but who is a talented escape artist and climber. She enjoys the garden and was house-trained from day one. Her eating habits are questionable, and we have to compete with her when opening cupboards, or the fridge. The dog and she have become a tag-team for stealing food. She is very skilled at this, much to the dog's delight. She licks everyone that comes into the house to visit, and occasionally has to be removed from our guests' laps after they have endured her grooming them for ten minutes. She particularly likes beards. As we speak she is lying on her back, in a disused brown cardboard box by the Christmas tree. She has a full belly and a smile on her face. That pretty much sums up her new life here.'

Elke commented: 'I am very happy to know that the cat is in good hands. Thinking about the whole thing now, I have some comments to say: Now that I know how the transport and papers for the UK for animals work, I would probably do it again, because in the beginning nobody knew how different everything is to the UK in contrast with other European countries. I would recommend Catsnip pass on this information and give the appropriate addresses – for example, Mark's in Rome – so that people know what they have to do. He knows every rule of every country for import and export of animals, and was a huge help for me. With the right information it is not too difficult to get things done but it takes some time and patience.'

And money! Sadie ended up with a £3,000 bill. As she said: 'It's such a shame that there is not a revised/alternative way to bring rescue animals to other parts of Europe. It actually disgusts me that all the money I have paid has gone to BA, rather than as a donation to Oscar or a cat rescue organisation in Sicily. I'm imagining that £3,000 would have paid for quite a few cats to be treated/spayed. Morally, in such circumstances as this, I feel that it's abhorrent to make fees so high. No wonder no one is willing to go through this. I would have been so much happier if I knew that airlines/organisations would waive some of their fees (VAT at least) to donate it so that the issue in Sicily could be addressed. There are so many people who would be willing to help if the cost wasn't so vast. It's just been so ridiculous that I'm furious that this system hasn't been changed. Nothing is given towards raising awareness in Sicily or towards rescue organisations.'

I thoroughly agree, Sadie, but rejoice that there are people like you and Eddie who care.

THIRTY-SEVEN

I Come to Terms with Sicily

Another year has passed and autumn has come round again. Once again I am back in Sicily.

The first chestnuts of the season, their shiny, charred coats splitting to reveal the creamy coloured meat within. Prosecco in crystal, fluted glasses, a vase of perfect pink roses… It looks like a still life painting. We are in Umberto Martorana's apartment at the end of the Corso. He has invited me for a drink and to talk about the Taormina of once upon a time.

The building is unremarkable from the outside; it does not prepare you for the gem within. Every aspect is carefully chosen and exquisite, from the Sicilian enamels in his bedroom to the alabaster busts against the walls, the pictures in his elegant living room. Beautiful carpets lie on the polished wood floors – a proper setting for such a cultivated man. He paints. His pictures are deceptively simple: two countrywomen against a frieze of olive trees, a shrine to the Madonna crowded with simple offerings, water reflecting the multicolours of a fishing boat – quintessentially Sicilian. He travels. From the books precisely placed around this room I gather he is also an extensive reader.

He has promised to show me his photograph albums, the images of lords and ladies, actors and writers, socialites – memories of another, more elegant Taormina, a time of fancy dress parties and dinners, cocktails at expat villas and visiting yachts.

Those were the disappearing years of a belle epoque that reigned at the end of the nineteenth, beginning of the twentieth centuries: an idyllic time.

It was at the Hotel Vittorio in 1891 Oscar Wilde took a room. Thirty-seven years old, he had left his wife to embrace his true sexuality, which would lead to imprisonment and forced labour. The literary genius would be ostracised and live out his last miserable years in Paris.

In those early years of the twentieth century, the best touring companies in Sicily played spectacles and operettas at the Greek theatre. The cabarets had a fatal influence on the nobility from Catania who, falling for a pair of lovely legs, gambled their marriages and inheritances. Some were reduced by their impossible and violent passion to commit suicide in a hotel room and often, to save Taormina's face, they were hurriedly dispatched.

Closing the albums, I sign Umberto's famous visitors book. I sip my Prosecco and nibble those first chestnuts of autumn. They seem somehow significant: mature fruit but containing spring and summer. I feel I have made a long journey and now come 'home' as I sit in Umberto's peaceful apartment, the sounds of the Corso far away. It is as if, this evening, all the long negotiations with Sicily have ended and we have reached a kind of truce, even though it can never be more than an uneasy one. A balance has been restored and, once again, I can see not only the shadows but the sunshine as well.

In the morning I go down to Isola Bella and gaze at that view as if I cannot take it in enough. I gaze and gaze. Light permeates everything, piercing the heat haze that shrouds the bay, the spume that fans out behind a boat. It illuminates another pagan world, tranquil and joyful. It is what one yearns for during those grey days in Northern Europe, to be made alive again by the light. I can understand how it is that Emilio paints and paints this scene yet again. There is another quality about Sicily, which he once described to me. He related how he took an Englishman – a man who was not accustomed to expressing his feelings – to stand at the top of Isola Bella.

'He was enchanted and turned to me and said, "You can touch the air."'

As I wander over the isthmus and back, I think of all those times when leaving the place, this small island in the Mediterranean, I would pause and gaze down Isola Bella, committing it to my memory. Isola Bella has been a recurring theme in my life in Sicily as it has Elke's.

That September day, she was in reminiscent mood: 'My first footsteps into Sicily were in the town of Messina. My future husband, Marquis Emilio Bosurgi, took me from Rome to Messina in a *wagon lit* sleeping car – a long trip from Rome to Sicily at that time. When we arrived at the train station of Messina I was extremely disappointed. I had imagined the island of Sicily similar to the Caribbean with sandy beaches, palm trees and hot weather. Nothing like that:

Messina was ugly, the weather grey and cold (February) and no Hula-Hula girls, no white sand beaches with palm trees.

'But Emilio said: "Wait and see when we get to Taormina, everything will be different." We took his Alfa-Romeo sports car to Taormina, parked on the road in front of a little island called Isola Bella. To get to it we had to climb down a steep staircase to a stony beach, walk along it until we reached the narrowest distance between land and island. Emilio told me to put on long rubber boots and to follow him slowly, walking through rather high water and waves. But I did not put my feet firmly enough on the ground and the next big wave just knocked me over. Here I was in the icy-cold water, Emilio grabbed me by my hair and I got back on my feet. Thank God I had a suitcase with dry clothes, which was carried by a servant on his head, so it would not get wet!

'Here we were on this mysterious little island. I was soaking wet and Emilio was having the largest laugh about my first meeting with the Sicilian sea. There was a nice chimney in the house on top of the island and I changed my clothes and dried the wet stuff at the nice cosy fire. We had good Sicilian wine and Emilio cooked a huge steak.

'Next morning: what a surprise, no more strong wind, no more heavy sea, but the most beautiful sunshine instead, and the flat sea had a violet-blue colour. What a change from yesterday! It was a breathtakingly beautiful atmosphere. Unfortunately I had to go back to work in Germany, but on my next vacation in summer I was back in Taormina and after a year I gave up my job and moved to Sicily. From then on most of the time I spent on Isola Bella, taking care of Emilio's customers and friends, showing them the island and inviting them for lunch.

'Slowly, Emilio constructed many rooms on the island, one for each member of the family. Every room had a bathroom, a chimney and a little corner to boil tea or coffee. Many times I was angry because he spent all his free time with his workers constructing new places and studying a method so as not to ruin the original look of the island. Everything was made to look like little caves, with the walls carefully covered with the natural rocks of the island. The result was to create a unique work of art from nature.

'It was the happiest time of my life,' she continued. 'We lived a wonderful twenty years, and really loved it, doing a big favour to the town of Taormina. Then it was requisitioned and we had to leave this corner of paradise. It fell into dilapidation.'

Maybe one day Isola Bella will return to its original beauty. Nevertheless, it will never forget those splendid years when all those important personages walked on her in admiration.

Coming from different backgrounds, though both lovers of this beautiful island, somehow Elke and I were brought together by our love of cats and our desire to give them happier lives. But our affection for Sicily is tempered by the fight to rescue its felines; there is still a long way to go.

I think of those words of D.H. Lawrence as he and Frieda prepared to leave Taormina in 1923. They sat with their luggage packed up, ready to leave Villa Fontana Vecchia.

'My heart is trembling with pain – the going away from home and the people and Sicily. Perhaps Frieda is right and we shall return to our Fontana. I don't say no. I don't say anything for certain. Today I go – tomorrow I return. So things go.'

So things go. I will return.

ADDENDUM

A Practical Chapter

*I*t is now twelve years since the day Andrew and I found that badly injured black and white cat. Although, like many other tourists, I had fed stray cats for a long time before that, this was my first experience of dealing with such an emergency. I learned the hard way and have continued to learn ever since.

I've learned, for example, to distinguish between the cat with a cosy home and loving owner and the feline that has never known anything other than life on the streets. As Guy, my wonderful UK vet, has said, the welfare of these feral animals is paramount and above human feelings, a question of doing what is best for them rather than being sentimental. This might sound harsh and it is sometimes difficult to carry out. Unlike their domesticated cousins, these *randagi* don't have anyone who will nurse them through a lengthy and possibly complicated period of treatment or disabilities that make leading a normal life possible. Even if they are lucky and receive some first aid, their ultimate fate will be to survive on their own. You have to decide whether this might cause them distress and danger at not being able to defend themselves.

The eye disease I've mentioned earlier is rife among kittens in Sicily. If it's not treated in time, this ultimately leads to blindness. The question has to be asked: is it right to allow these small creatures to struggle for an existence in their feral world if there is not an assured source of regular food? They may not be able to scavenge and will therefore die a miserable death.

Unlike pet cats, which often don't get on with other felines, feral colonies frequently develop naturally. These are usually made up of groups of related females and the size of colony is directly related to the availability of food, water and shelter. Cats are extremely resourceful creatures and can adapt to many different habitats.

Those within the colony recognise each other by sharing their scent through rubbing against each other. Although they appear close, they are not completely reliant upon the others and will hunt and eat alone. If an unfamiliar cat intrudes on their territory, they will soon see it off. After neutering, a feral cat should be released back into its territory as quickly as possible – this is so the cat will not lose the communal scent and end up being rejected by other cats in the colony.

As I came to understand this, I learned another valuable lesson: only in rare circumstances should you remove a cat from its colony or indeed relocate the entire colony.

Relocation of feral cats is extremely stressful for them, as they become very dependent on the familiarity of their own environment. Neither should they be released just anywhere. An appropriate habitat needs to be found and the cats require a period of adjustment while they learn where they can find food and shelter. Most often, there is no reason to remove them from their habitats. Ferals become well adapted to their territory and can live safely and contentedly in alleyways, parking lots, vacant lots, backyards and a host of other locations – urban, suburban and rural. Yet another consideration: if all or most of the cats are neutered, taking them somewhere else can create a vacuum. Other unneutered cats may move into the area and start the cycle all over again.

I made a bad mistake before I understood this. It happened during a neutering trip in Letojanni as I did the rounds with my trap, traipsing up and down streets and out into the countryside in an amazing November heat. I found a mother and her kittens in the derelict remains of an empty house close to a busy exit roundabout and was terrified the young ones might run under a passing car. A friend agreed to take them in her car to what we believed to be a safe place in the country. In doing so, we removed them from their known source of food and water, and reports came back that they had died. It was totally the wrong thing to do and I regret it to this day. Just another example of confusing feral with domesticated cats.

Remember my experience with Lizzie and my first encounter with a feral cat? She was anxious and fearful, her one desire to escape. Of course, she didn't understand I was trying to help her. It is really not advisable to try to socialise a grown feral cat. If you are prepared to devote time and attention, however, you can work with young feral kittens and persuade them to become affectionate and loving companions. It's not something that will happen overnight but can be a rewarding experience. Yes, it's possible to transform a spitting, hissing ball of fluff, but the time it takes depends on their age. Just about anyone can socialise a kitten that is eight weeks or younger. Those between two and four months of age often demand more time and skill.

There are really no set rules as each kitten will learn at a different rate and thus become accustomed to you. Be patient.

When tourists contact me for help with a small and apparently lost kitten, my first question is always: 'Are you certain the mother isn't around?' The kitten may have simply strayed or the mother is keeping herself from view. It is also a good idea to check whether the cats are being fed by a *gattara*, a cat lady, in case she feels some sense of ownership. That was Dawn's dilemma when she spotted Lionel. As she told me: 'We were having a much-needed holiday but it was somewhat spoilt by seeing this poor little ginger and white cat sitting outside someone's gate. He had scratched himself bald in places and seemed to have a coloured liquid drooling from his mouth. We passed him every time we went into town and, as cat lovers with a thoroughly spoilt feline at home, we felt we must do something. However, we couldn't be sure that the person we saw feeding other cats might object if we took him away. We got as far as contacting the vet but then, because we don't speak Italian, were nervous of creating a confrontation. Reluctantly, we had to abandon the idea.'

Although no one actually possesses a feral cat, it is courtesy to first check with the *gattara* and tell her what you intend to do rather than taking command. Often she will be pleased that someone else is prepared to pay for treatment.

From time to time, the local authorities in tourist towns such as Taormina try to make it an offence to feed feral cats. In my experience, I have never found an enforcement of fines. Just make sure you clean up any leftover scraps and wash plates or bowls – important in a hot climate. Cats are clean creatures; it is we humans who, by leaving the site messy, give them the reputation of being 'dirty'.

Never, under any circumstances, give a cat milk to drink. Felines are lactose intolerant and it will give them diarrhoea. Water is their natural and best drink.

It is very difficult to catch a feral cat without a trap; they will scratch and bite to evade capture and a bite from a cat can be very nasty indeed. If you are visiting Sicily, you may be lucky in finding someone who has one of these humane traps. They are simple to set, with food placed at the far end; as the cat enters and moves forward, a spring mechanism is released and shuts the door. If you are living in Sicily, you might want to invest in one or more. Metalcote is an excellent UK company that supplies these at a reasonable price and will deliver overland. I've been a customer for years, and also for cages including the crush cage. Sounds alarming, but it isn't in reality. A lever mechanism reduces the size of the cage, bringing the feline closer to the bars, and makes it easy to give medication or anaesthetic.

Naturally, these feral cats resent being captured and put up a lot of fuss. Always cover the trap or cage with an old towel or small blanket to shut out light and quieten the captive – and get them to the vet as speedily as possible.

There is a great deal of indifference towards animals in the south of Italy as well as Sicily. There is an argument that these regions have more financial problems than those of the north. In my opinion, it has a lot more to do with education or the absence of it, and lack of understanding of animals as sentient beings capable of feeling the same fear, pain and hunger as we do. They also need affection and give so much in return. Instead, I've seen parents warning their children to keep away from a cat or dog so that the youngsters grow up with the same attitude and so the chain continues.

Survival is the key word when speaking of colonies of feral cats. Not for them the toys and treats of many domestic cats, including my beloved Sheba. Essentially, it is based on scavenging for food and, in the case of unneutered cats, reproducing. Because of this there is a risk of their suffering from FIV, feline immunodeficiency virus. FIV and HIV are both lentiviruses but humans cannot be infected by FIV, nor can HIV infect cats. This feline disease is transmitted primarily through saliva bites such as those incurred during territorial fights between males. Since many feral cats are unneutered and have to compete for food, there is a higher incidence of FIV in such felines. Transmission between cats in a group who do not fight is unlikely as the virus can only survive a very brief time outside a cat's body, and it cannot be transmitted indirectly, such as on food, feeding equipment, clothes, shoes, hands, etc. (unlike the situation with feline leukaemia). FIV infects many cell types in a cat. Although it can often be tolerated well, it may eventually lead to weakening the immune system. Domestic cats are much less likely to be infected unless they come into contact with infected cats. In retrospect, I think that was the cause of my beloved Fluffy's illness and eventual death. At that time I wasn't aware of the possibility of FIV but I've since seen its signs in the many feral cats I have encountered. They may suffer from diarrhoea or conjunctivitis. Other common signs are gingivitis (gum inflammation), sneezing, snuffling, a discharge from the nose or eyes, or kidney failure. Unfortunately, love and care are not usually the lot of these cats as with the domestic puss. But a neuter programme can have a threefold benefit: controlling the population, enabling a more plentiful supply of food among fewer cats and reducing the tendency to fight.

Although you cannot contract FIV through contact with feral cats, you should obviously take care in handling them. As I've written earlier, many of these felines are shy, even fearful of human beings and view any approach as a threat. Unless you are reasonably sure they welcome your overtures – as in the case of Sadie and Katarina – it is wise not to try to grab them with your bare hands. Their natural response will be to scratch or even bite. It is the reason we've always used the humane trap during the Catsnip trips. If you are thinking of making cat rescue an ongoing venture, then invest in the tough gauntlets sold by companies like MDC Exports Ltd.

It never ceases to anger me when I hear a parent tell a child: 'Don't touch that animal, you will catch a disease.' Most diseases that infect cats can only be spread from cat to cat, not from cat to human. You are much more likely to catch an infectious disease from the person standing next to you at a bus stop than from a feline. And yet the catch and kill advocates of 'controlling' feral cat populations defend themselves with these untruths. The only possible carrier of a disease could be in the cat's faeces and normal hygiene dictates you wouldn't be likely to touch that. The belief that feral cats spread rabies is another vacuous argument; the risk of catching this dreaded disease from these felines is almost non-existent. Trap/neuter/return is also a safeguard against rabies because they will also be vaccinated, ensuring that cats in managed colonies cannot catch or spread this disease. As for the notion that cats will unexpectedly leap out of alleyways and bite children, it is just as nonsensical as it sounds. Sicily, like Britain, is now officially rabies-free, although, according to wildlife writer and preservationist Vincenzo Mormino, the rare red fox may sometimes be infected. A timid and human-fearing animal, it is rarely, if ever seen. Nevertheless, anyone who wishes to transport a cat into the UK must be sure it has had the appropriate anti-rabies immunisation.

Over more recent years, I've been encouraged by the discovery of several Italian animal welfare organisations, such as OIPA and ENPA. I've also come across some wonderful dedicated individuals. Valeria and her valiant band of volunteers have a daily struggle with the influx of animals dumped outside the doors of their refuge. Their battle is a formidable one and they need all the support we can give them. Some town hall departments recognise the problem of feral over-population and have agreements with a local vet. That's what Helen discovered with her tiny kitten, Gavroche, once she had persuaded the police to help her. Others choose to do nothing about it. As a tourist, it will depend on where you are staying, whether you can expect any help. There remains a great deal to be done to raise awareness and create an on-going programme of trap, neuter and return. My dream of a mobile unit and the funds to run an on-going trap/neuter/return programme remains a long way from being fulfilled.

During my Catsnip years, I have been accused of 'going against nature', even being 'a cat murderer'. In a Roman Catholic country like Sicily, there are inevitably those who see spaying and neutering as a violation of God's law. But those same people turn a blind eye to the female cats, which have kittens continually until they are worn out, and the sickly kittens that fall prey to terrible eye disease. They choose not to know about their fellow humans' cruelty and indifference. Yes, I've had my moments of doubt when I've wondered if I was doing the right thing but then you consider that a feral cat can produce three litters of kittens a year, with an average of four to eight kittens. In seven years, one female cat and her offspring can theoretically produce 420,000 cats!

Not all of them will survive, of course, but what of the number who do? The humane solution is trap, neuter and return. If only the authorities could see it that way! The Sicilian bureaucracy is a curious thing with many regulations but these are not adhered to, according to a local animal lover I spoke to recently. I had asked him if he could check on Dawn's cat Lionel.

It's certain that I can expect nothing helpful from the vets of ASL (state vets), whom I have already contacted many times. Their reply is always the same: that the town hall must decide to make a payment of 300 euros, otherwise they won't neuter. This is something with which I am battling because the Sicilian Regional law no. 281/91 for the prevention of stray animals states clearly that they must neuter and microchip at zero cost, but they don't do it. In the case of accidents or the cat should be admitted for treatment, there is no structure in place.

Faced with this situation, tourists search the Internet and, you've guessed it, they find Catsnip. Several times their emails have ended with 'and I've fallen in love with her and would like to bring her back to the UK'. At that point I hold up my hand and say, that is a knee-jerk reaction. You are on holiday and probably not thinking in the rational way you might at home. Look at the facts and think it through. The process of bringing an animal back to the UK, while not as lengthy as it used to be, is a big undertaking both in terms of time and money. But as Sadie proved, with love and determination it can be done.

Useful Contacts

CATSNIP

Its aims are: To pursue a catch/neuter/return programme of feral cats in Sicily on a longer term and to alter the mindset of local people, particularly young people. To attempt to persuade them to see animals as sentient beings capable of the same feelings as human beings and also with needs and rights, which should be respected, particularly because they cannot speak for themselves. To gain permission to take vets to Sicily on an official basis for catch/neuter/return sessions. To address the running of kennels and catteries in tourist areas, where animals live in atrocious conditions.

Email: info@catsnip.org.uk

Website: www.catsnip.org.uk

ANIMALS WORLDWIDE

The charity seeks to build relationships with travel companies and to harness the eyes, ears and energies of the travelling public to identify both good and bad practice. AWW believes that it is in the interest of both the industry and of animal welfare that we recognise and seek to exploit this opportunity to make real progress.

Website: www.animalsworldwide.org

CARE4CATS

An English charity, founded by animal lover Angela Collins in 1999. Her aim: to care for and humanely reduce the number of stray cats in Ibiza. Catch/neuter/return trips annually.

Website: www.care4cats.org.uk

CATS IN ITALY

Kathy T. Hisamatsu's personal blog about cat rescue volunteering. Intended for adopters, volunteers and cat guardians living in Italy.

Website: www.catsinitaly.com

ENPA

The oldest of the larger animal welfare associations in Italy. Its aims are protection of animals and caring for nature and the environment. It promotes animal rights and also offers an education programme in schools of every grade.

Website: www.enpa.it

GREEK CAT WELFARE SOCIETY

The Society was formed in 1992. Its aim is to undertake neutering of colonies of stray cats and in doing so educate and encourage local people to also have their animals neutered. TNR is carried out on a regular basis several times a year.

Website: www.greekcatwelfare.moonfruit.com

IL GATTILE TRIESTE

The association was created with the aim of controlling the birth rate of, caring for and effecting adoption of street cats. In addition, it aims to raise awareness and respect for felines among local people and, in particular, young people.

Website: www.ilgattile.it

L'OASIS FELINA

This feline sanctuary was created in 2000 with the aims of helping feral and abandoned cats, providing food veterinary care, a home where they can have a cosy bed to sleep in amid the company of other cats.

Website: www.ilgattile.it

OIPA ITALIA ONLUS

Its aims are the guardianship of nature and the environment, the abolition of vivisection in countries throughout the world, and the defence of animals from whatever form of maltreatment: hunting, circus animals, bull fights, popular festival with animals, feral animals, traffic of exotic animal zoos, intensive rearing, slaughterhouses, and to encourage vegan and vegetarian diets.

Email: info@oipa.org
Website: www.oipa.org

METALCOTE

Manufactures and supplies plastic-coated cat baskets, wire pet carriers, mesh cages and animal traps. It also provides many animal aids to vets, such as end-opening restrainer-trapping cages for administering injections, or rescue traps, for the capture and transportation of wild feral animals and small rodents and birds.
Email: sales@metalcote.co.uk
Website: www.metalcote.co.uk

SNIP INTERNATIONAL

A UK registered charity dedicated to improving standards of animal welfare around the world. In particular, SNIP International promotes neutering programmes aimed at stray and feral animals. It respects life and does not endorse destruction of healthy animals.
Website: www.snip-international.org

SPANA

The Society for the Protection of Animals Abroad is a leading charity for working animals worldwide and the communities they support: 'We know that working animals are essential to the health and economic wellbeing of millions of vulnerable families across the developing world. But often these hardworking animals lack access to even basic care: that's where we come in.'
Website: www.spana.org

Acknowledgements

My heartfelt thanks go to:

Elke Bosurgi, untiring cat lady and dear friend

Oscar La Manna, guardian of Sicily's feline waifs and strays and wonderful colleague

Guy Liebenberg, vet in a million

Animals' Voice, which supports small projects like Catsnip

Mario Pavone, wise commentator on Sicily

Valeria Cundari, defender of animal rights

Nigel and Marit, Elizabeth, Barbara, Joy and all whose donations have made this work possible

Kathy, dear colleague and translator of cat behaviour

Andrew, dear companion and navigator on this endeavour

My beloved cat, Sheba, constant writing companion and stress buster

And all the cats and cat ladies I have had the pleasure of knowing.

Glossary

A domani: 'See you tomorrow'

Briscola: an Italian trick-taking card game

Cassata or *Cassata Siciliana*: a traditional dessert from the Palermo and Messina areas. It can also refer to ice cream studded with candied or dried fruit and nuts

Domani domani: 'Tomorrow, always tomorrow'

Freddo da fa morire: cold enough to freeze you to death

Micio: puss or pussycat

Panna cotta: literally, 'cooked cream'. A dessert made with thick cream, egg white and honey

Passeggiata: literally, a walk but often a stroll with friends in a public street or square

Roba da donne: women's stuff

Salotta: living room

Sott'olio: pickled in oil

Trovatelle: foundlings